gesture
and
response

gesture
and
response

25 buildings by
william pedersen
of KPF architects

ORO

ORO Editions — Novato, California

ORO Editions
Publishers of Architecture, Art, and Design
Gordon Goff: Publisher

www.oroeditions.com
info@oroeditions.com

Published by ORO Editions

Foreword and Texts by William Pedersen
Managing Editor: Jake Anderson

Book Design by Pablo Mandel
Cover Concept by William Pedersen
Typeset in Akzidenz Grotesk

10 9 8 7 6 5 4 3 2 1   First Edition

ISBN 978-1-943532-30-8

Color Separations and Printing: ORO Group Ltd.
Printed in China.

ORO Editions makes a continuous effort to minimize the overall carbon footprint of its
publications. As part of this goal, ORO Editions, in association with Global ReLeaf, arranges to
plant trees to replace those used in the manufacturing of the paper produced for its books. Global
ReLeaf is an international campaign run by American Forests, one of the world's oldest nonprofit
conservation organizations. Global ReLeaf is American Forests' education and action program
that helps individuals, organizations, agencies, and corporations improve the local and global
environment by planting and caring for trees.

"To the memory of Elizabeth,
my beloved wife of 60 years,
and to our daughters Kia and Lea."

Contents

Introduction

Forty-four years ago, on the eve of our national bicentennial, Gene Kohn, Shelley Fox, and I began our collaboration. Each of us brought a very different personality type to our partnership. Based on our individual strengths, we each focused on a specific aspect of making architecture. Together we possessed the abilities necessary to create an architectural firm that could aspire to buildings of the highest quality, creating designs that captured the condition of our times.

I have often compared our partnership to the components of a sailboat: the keel, the hull, and the sails. Gene, while a former designer himself, was the entrepreneurial force of the firm, always leading us to new opportunities. Shelley was our stabilizing force, administering the complexities of our office. Through my example, not my words, I set the design direction for the office. Knowing that we had the components necessary to become a large office, doing many buildings simultaneously, I rejected the role of "director of design." If we were to grow stronger with each succeeding generation, we needed to encourage our most talented and determined young designers to develop into design leaders themselves, capable of initiating work that reinforced our collective goals. Younger designers would be raised in our culture. None were to be imported. We embarked on a modular form of growth—with each design principal acting as a creative module—this has proven successful over the years. It was an early decision on our part, one that we have never come to regret. Our resolve promoted an energetic and positive form of internal competition, and a dynamic that inspired everyone to achieve his or her full architectural potential.

Our collective mission, which came about slowly over time, was not the product of a polemical manifesto. It evolved organically from the opportunities we created as we focused on designing the fundamental building blocks of the modern city. No building type is more dominant, or pervasive, than the commercial high-rise office building. It is ubiquitous now throughout the world. By its nature it is insular and autonomous. We wanted to find ways of bringing it into a more social interchange with other urban structures, inspiring connections and linkages in the fabric of the modern city.

My professional career began when I had the great fortune to work closely, for four years, with I.M. Pei in New York. I.M. had been on my Rome Prize jury and he suggested I might join his office when I returned from Rome. In 1967 I did. Had I not, my career would have been very different. It was in the office of I.M. Pei and Partners that I was first exposed to the focus and dedication required to make architecture of the highest quality. I also developed huge respect for the contributions of supporting architects and consultants who each contributed to the diverse challenges of building significant architecture. Without a highly coordinated team willing to master every detail of construction, the quality of architecture to which I.M. aspired was not possible.

I.M. had both the temperament and talent associated with architects of genius, but I found that I.M. was not solitary in his creativity. By contrast, I recall Louis Kahn telling a story of doing a drawing as a child. His father, as he watched him, offered a suggestion and added it to the drawing. Kahn tore up the paper saying, "It is no longer mine." I assume he felt the same way about his architecture. I.M. worked in a very different manner. He encouraged contributions from his team. He made each of us feel good about our contributions—when they were good. It was his example of design leadership I wanted to follow during my career. He always let the best ideas prevail, regardless of their authorship.

Another key turning point arrived in 1970 with a telephone call from Gene Kohn. I had not met Gene before. He was calling at the suggestion of James Nash, a former colleague of mine in the Pei office, who had recently joined Gene in the office of John Carl Warnecke and Associates in New York. Gene asked if I would be interested in joining that firm, of which he had become the president. At the time I was deeply engaged in the design of the National Gallery in Washington, D.C., with I.M. and his team. I was greatly enjoying the experience, and benefitting from all I was learning of I.M.'s working method. I was soon to learn a very important thing about Gene—he never gives up. A year later he called again. It had been three years since I had started working on the Gallery and the design of the East Building was well along. Gene offered me the opportunity to design independently—with a team and a client of my own. I took it. It was the beginning of a 50-year professional relationship, founded on profound mutual respect, which made possible all that followed in my career.

The first design assignment I was given was a massive academic structure on the City College of New York campus in Upper Manhattan. During the process of designing this project I developed the working method—I call it "the comparative process"—which I have used for the last 50 years. But it was failure that bred the process. And it brought me into another 50-year relationship with a young man, assigned to my team and not even out of architecture school, who was to eventually become a leading design partner at KPF and a close friend—William Louie.

In my first design presentation to the CCNY client I presented, as I.M. would do, a single design solution. (Previously, I had never even presented a design to a client, let alone to one as aggressive and as complex as the client I was about to encounter.) The presentation went badly. My design, about which I was enthusiastic, was brutally rejected. Warnecke was furious. The commission itself was endangered. I needed to develop an alternate strategy. Instead of presenting a single design which implied a thumbs-up/thumbs-down response from the client—I would, in our next meeting, present several different approaches to the design. However, they were not to be presented as a Chinese menu of alternatives from which the client could make the choice. I presented them instead as a means of discovering, for both the client and myself, the aspirations for the project that we jointly held. Of course, I had strong opinions about the merits of each. But it was through the comparison of the alternative approaches that I intended to bring us, together, to the solution.

The strategy succeeded. I was able to bring the clients into the process with me. In the discussion that followed I learned more about their vision, and they learned about mine. We became a team. Together we created a design environment in which the best ideas survived by mutual agreement. Internally, our teamwork was inclusive and energizing, and, to my mind, it became the key to elevating our collective design to a very high level...and doing it consistently. It was also critical to building an architectural firm in which talented people would want to remain throughout their careers.

What then are the "forces" fundamental to the designs we have accomplished over these many years? There are three: the site, the program, and the client. The first two are highly specific to each design. But so is the third. Many of our clients have been developers. Each of them have big teams assembled to manage the many aspects of the construction process. Much has been written about the loss of the architect's position as "master builder." I do not see it as a loss but as a gain. The scale of our buildings requires the expertise of many. Making architecture of great size and complexity requires the architect to acknowledge and respect the various disciplines that contribute to the design process. It also requires that the architect have an in-house team with a balance of expertise and experience allowing the architects to interface with consultants necessary to build these complex structures. Over the years, assembling teams capable of enabling a highly professional execution of our projects has been one of our proudest accomplishments. We intend to build well. We intend to serve our clients well. That requires an attitude toward building that is more than just about design. Building well requires enormous persistence and expertise. While the direction of our individual designs throughout the years has often been challenged, the quality of the execution of our buildings has always been respected.

Were I asked to capture in words my dominant architectural aspiration I would say it is "creating connections." Making visual connections and linkages, particularly when designing urban buildings, has always been my point of departure. Any site, regardless of whether it's urban, suburban, or rural, offers clues for linkages if you look for them. The ability, and the desire, to be able to "read" a site for these clues is one of an architect's most necessary skills. But the skill cannot be developed if it is not sought.

Historically, the fabric of linkages among buildings in traditional cities was based on a common architectural language and scale. Buildings agreed on how to meet the earth, the sky, and each other. Within a connected urban fabric, the exceptional was made even more so by a constructed backdrop that enabled the best to dominate. Over the last 80 years, that urban scenario has been lost. Now great buildings mostly arise, not as the exceptions within a prevailing norm, as exceptions among other exceptions.

During the late '70s and early '80s, I went through a period when I felt we might look to the transitional era between classicism and modernism for clues, in an effort to inspire urban linkage with tall buildings. Rockefeller Center in New York inspired me. However, my attempt was not fruitful. Unless all others built with similar aspirations, attempting to turn back the clock was futile.

Tall buildings have anthropomorphic characteristics that encourage me to think of them as human participants in the city. For a social gathering to be successful everyone must engage in animated conversation; so must buildings of the modern city. Despite the differences in their dress and their character, all must gesture to each other. Like actors in a play, their gestural dialogue determines the success of the performance. Gesture is possible with buildings. Architecture has the capacity to physically respond to context by reaching out to establish linkages. Overt gesture is possible between buildings even among those with different styles of expression. If the common language of dress and character of a traditional city is not achievable or even desirable within the modern city, a gestural response in physical form is.

Throughout the early part of KPF's history, speculative high-rise office buildings dominated our practice. I was determined to design them so they achieved urban connections through formal gesture. Each city we worked in offered different external clues. In time, and with globalism, the pressures of the immediate external context coalesced with issues of regional architectural character. A building in Chicago needs to be of a different character than one in New York. And, as our practice became global, one in North America had to be very different from one in Europe and certainly one in Asia. Character and composition were the two indispensable ingredients of meaningful urban architecture. Each must contribute, each must derive from the qualities of a specific place.

In time our practice became known for the quality of execution we displayed in our commercial high-rise buildings. As a result, other building types came into the office. Suburban corporate headquarters, campus academic buildings, airports, U.S. federal courthouses, and even single-family houses broadened our range of architectural investigation. Besides the search for linkage and connection that emerged from our focus on speculative commercial high-rise buildings, we were able to factor in the programmatic intention of known users. The push and pull of internal and external forces became an enriching dynamic in our work. We were well suited to respond to the programmatic aspirations of our clients: we listened. We need to listen in order to creatively transform a building's program into meaningful architecture. It is a step-by-step process of first understanding and then converting the statistical pieces of an initial document into a physical result that manifests the full aspirations of a client—including those the client may not have earlier realized.

The documentation of buildings I designed over a 45-year period is the subject of this book. Each building was created in collaboration with colleagues under my design leadership. Several of my colleagues with whom I worked, then in the early stages of their careers, are still with us at KPF. Now they lead design teams of their own. Enabling talented and dedicated architects to find a path to achieving their lifetime professional goals has been an objective of our firm from the very beginning. It has enabled KPF to grow and to evolve. It might be our most significant accomplishment.

For this book I have selected twenty-five of my projects done over this period. They are chronologically listed beginning with 333 Wacker Drive in Chicago and ending with Hudson Yards in New York. For each I tell the story of our architectural intentions. Not told is the story of the dynamic between us, as architects, and the clients these buildings were designed for. Nor is the tale of the internal dynamic between me and members of my teams. Each story is important to the success of a particular building but requires a book in itself. Here, documentation of the architectural intentions behind each of the buildings is the primary focus.

Now a new generation leads KPF. Guided by James von Klemperer, our president, the dynamic of the office has become that of an energetic academy. Symposia, panel discussions, and lectures by outside experts and even some of our youngest staff happen all the time in our offices. All the challenges of the emerging era, particularly those of sustainability and craft, are being pursued with complete intensity by our global web of offices. We are working in a new era—one that combines the goals I have outlined in this book with those that have arisen in this new generation. It is a most exciting, and urgent time to be an architect.

William Pedersen

333 Wacker Drive

Chicago, Illinois, U.S. – 1982

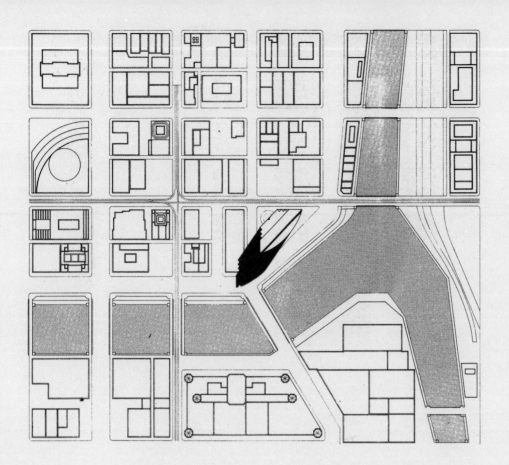

Site plan

Two years after we started Kohn Pedersen Fox, my partner, Gene Kohn, received a call from Thomas Klutznick, the president of Urban Investment in Chicago. He wanted our help in developing a site on Wacker Drive, at the bend of the Chicago River, north of the city's commercial center. Klutznick hoped to attract ABC Television to his building by providing them studio space in the base of a high-rise commercial office structure. Since KPF had designed studios for ABC near Lincoln Center in New York, he felt we might be able to help him bring them to Chicago and his building.

His triangular site, 333 Wacker Drive, is directly across from the famous Merchandise Mart, a huge 4,000,000 sq.ft. Art Deco stone structure finished in 1930 (at that time it was the biggest building in the world). Until the 1950s the Chicago River, flowing out to Lake Michigan, was considered the northern edge of the commercial core of the city. The urban structures, which defined the sides of the river, were mostly built before, and soon after, the Great Depression. Together they created a predominantly masonry wall of buildings along its length. Our site was geometric punctuation in the wall. It was unusually prominent because of its location at the river's bend, adjacent to an elevated rail structure that brought commuters across the river into Chicago from the surrounding suburbs. It was a gateway to the city.

On my first visit to the site, the idea of a specific architectural response gesturing to the site immediately struck me. I have never had that happen, before or since. The bend in the Chicago River is a powerful urban event. The movement of the river pivots around the site. How could one not respond to its rotation? Rarely does a site speak with such clarity when one searches for an architectural response. Furthermore, the triangular geometry of the site made the building's shape almost unavoidable. Holding firm to the property lines on the two lateral sides leading into city fabric while celebrating the third side fronting the river seemed imperative. For that exceptional side we proposed an outwardly curving surface following the river's bend.

Kevin Lynch, in his influential book "The Image of the City," wrote about the orienting role of urban structures that provoke in the viewer's mind "imageability" and a better sense of "wayfinding." This pivotal site held the potential for fulfilling that urbanistic strategy. Here, a building could explain this part of Chicago's fabric, both on the ground and in the sky. It could become another strong urban marker in a city already made "imaginable" by many great buildings.

We showed our architectural response in a simple clay model to our future client on Gene's next visit to Chicago. He loved it so much that despite not being able to engage ABC, he risked building on this urban "outlier" site, asking us to lead the design. As a young emerging firm we were not yet fully capable of convincing our client we had the experience to handle both the design and the documentation of the project. Urban Investment engaged the excellent Chicago firm of Perkins and Will to join us as members of a team. Perkins+Will gave their unwavering support to our design intentions.

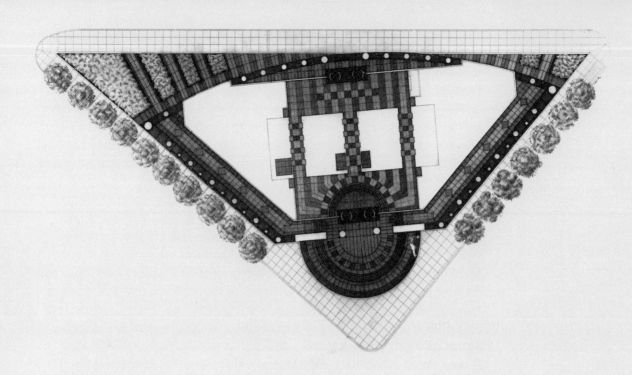

Ground-floor lobby plan

The image of an archer's bow, stretched taut by the cord, which joins its ends, has always captured me esthetically. Even more captivating is the dynamic of the bow immediately before the archer releases the arrow. Both of these images play a role in the design of 333 Wacker Drive. Given the tension before the release, the expectation for dramatic action is high. One experiences similar expectation just before a runner explodes from the starting blocks.

But beginning with a triangular building that curves outwardly on the dominant side was just a start. Several additional transformative steps were necessary. Far less obvious, but equally essential to the building's dynamic, is the slice taken from the belly of the curve as the structure reaches the sky. Two floors of mechanical services terminate the building. The full floor area was not needed. By intersecting the curve with a flat plane we juxtaposed a softly curving surface and the hard plane and created a dramatic termination of our bowing façade against the sky. The resulting shape, in plan, closely resembled that of an archer's bow stretched taut by its string. The energy of the gesture was further accentuated by dragging the planar slice down for several floors at the ends of the curve, interlocking and tensing the two geometries.

The geometric interplay of the building's form demanded a type of surface treatment that heightened its dynamic. The surface needed to be taut with a sense of being stretched and pulled, particularly on the great curving side. If properly tuned, this surface could dramatically register the changing quality of sunlight as it passes across the wall from morning to night. Reflective glass offered, to us, the greatest potential to optimize this daily transformation. We selected a green tint for a reason that could seem arbitrary if it hadn't worked so well—the water of the Chicago River has a distinctive greenish color.

Visually pulling the wall taut required a sense of it being horizontally tensioned. The neutrality of a grid of vertical and horizontal mullions, required to secure the glass, needed to be given a hierarchy enabling the horizontal to dominate. We accomplished this by making the horizontal mullions, at vertical six-foot centers, into a semicircular shape six inches in diameter. They are of brushed stainless steel. The vertical mullions, three inches in width and five feet apart, are almost flat to the glass and painted a dark brown. The resulting hierarchy created the illusion we sought.

Expressed as a weighty mass of stone—in contrast to the lightness of the glass volume above—the monumental base of the building is a product of contextual and programmatic requirements. It is horizontally banded with gray granite and green marble, enclosing a two-story mechanical room facing, only on one side, elevated train tracks carrying passengers to and from the city. The perimeter of this mechanical space, on the diagonal sides, is serrated in plan. These large serrations increase the surface area necessary to bring outside air into the fan rooms. They march along both of the diagonal sides of the building, giving it a more human scale. The serrations are each supported by octagonal columns, clad in black granite and green marble, forming a colonnade fronting onto glass enclosed

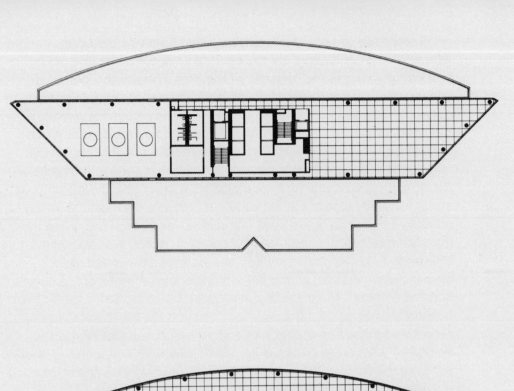

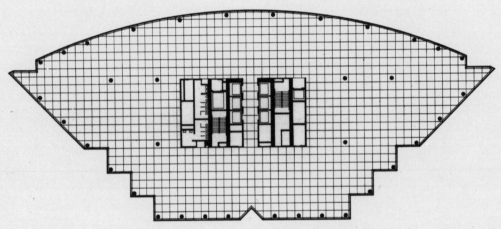

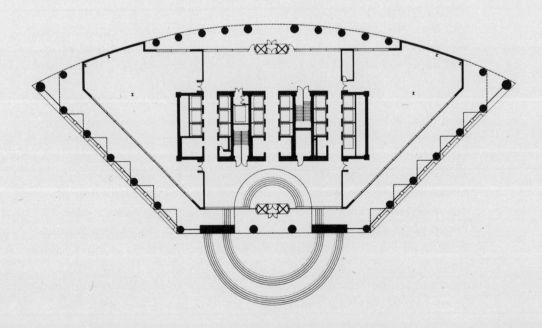

retail space on the ground level. Grand, decoratively detailed, circular air intakes, set in black granite panels, animate the serrated surface and give dignity and visual vitality to a mundane programmatic requirement necessary to the building's function. Carved into the curving riverside surface of the stone clad base and into its truncated side, facing the city, are portals of monumental scale leading to the entrance lobby. Here the exterior base materials are continued into the interior where they are further enhanced by crafted details creating a strong sense of invitation.

333 Wacker launched our career in the design of commercial office buildings. Completed in the early '80s, its success brought us many commissions of a similar type during the great building boom in the remainder of the decade. Finding alternative strategies for the successful urban participation of the high-rise commercial office building in the evolution of the modern city became the focus of our practice. Making the building a social participant in the city was our goal. This building initiated a strategy of contextual "gesture and response" I have used throughout my career.

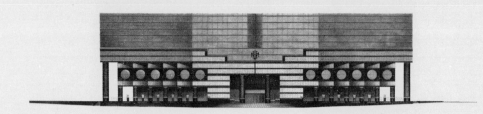

Base elevation drawings

DZ Bank
Headquarters

Frankfurt, Germany – 1993

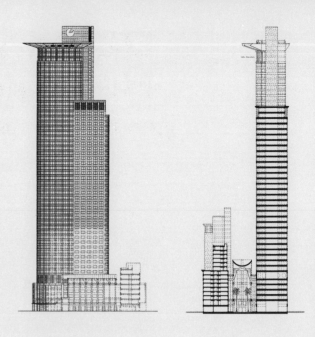

Site plan, east elevation, section, Bill's drawing

In the late fall of 1988 we were invited into a competition for the design of a new headquarters for the DZ Bank in Frankfurt, Germany, by the Dutch pension fund PGGM (which was serving as the Bank's owner representative). This would be my first opportunity to build in Germany and my first chance to work within the dimensional workplace requirements of the German building code, which requires workers to be in close proximity to natural light.

In the United States, the standard dimensional limitation, allowed by code, from the core of an office building to its outside wall was far greater than the seven-meter depth (22' 9") allowed in Germany. There, and in other European countries, working in natural light is a human right. In the United States, developers and clients encourage much greater dimensions in the interests of planning flexibility and construction economy: 45' is the standard. In the design of tall buildings, these internal dimensions make a substantial difference to the penetration of natural light into the workplace. Furthermore, they add the architectural challenge of dealing with bulky proportions.

Frankfurt, located on the river Main, is home to the European Central Bank and other major German financial institutions. The Mainzer Landstrasse, a central thoroughfare leading to Frankfurt's opera house, was to host the DZ Bank in close proximity to the Deutsche Bank. This important avenue had emerged as a commercial edge between the historic center of Frankfurt and a newer residential section to the north. The juxtaposition of these two districts played a fundamental role influencing our architectural response.

The bank's program, and the limited dimensions of the site, required a tall building. We were determined to mitigate the scale of the future structure by integrating it into the dynamics of the surrounding urban fabric. A series of datum elevations had emerged in the Frankfurt skyline over time as markers of the city's growth, and we intended to celebrate them in a design that acknowledged their significance.

The Mainzer Landstrasse's orientation to both the old city of Frankfurt, to the south, and to the newer postwar residential sector, to the north, influenced our design strategy. For years I had been looking for ways to enable our tall buildings to respond to the fabric of the city. For me, what emerged in Frankfurt was a fundamental breakthrough—a tall building composed of two volumes interlocking around a third in a type of fugue. In music the fugue is a compositional form that combines two or more voices about a central theme. Here, we proposed a tower of three parts, the tallest enclosing a core that bound the other two.

Before the initiation of our design, the height limit for towers in Frankfurt was 150 meters, and a generation of structures marked that height. Shortly before we entered the competition the limit was relaxed: we could go higher. We decided that we would represent the old height in our tower, while still going higher, and also weave other datum heights, dominant in other eras, into our design. The lower datum heights, of the traditional city, are represented in the

L-shaped structure that wraps two sides of the tower, forming a grand room, of civic proportions, around the tower. The two taller volumes of the tower, one in stone and one in glass, rise around the tower's core to unequal heights. The stone volume, rectangular in plan and 150 meters high (the former height limitation) faces and gestures to the residential fabric. The glass volume, 206 meters tall and curved in plan, faces the old city. It addresses it with a great cantilevered cornice—acting as a gesture offering, what can be interpreted as, an architectural benediction on the city.

Every external component of this complex responds to the contextual pressures surrounding it, especially at the corners of the site. Each corner engages a different condition. The three corners of the lower structure, anchored by vertical shafts, act like pivot points for the interpenetrating volumes that engage them. These shafts enclose vertical circulation. On the main façade, convex and concave forms, reminiscent of Baroque architecture, gesture in invitation to the Mainzer Landstrasse. The other façades mark key contextual heights of 25 and 50 meters.

Since the horizontal, floor by floor, stratification of tall buildings limits a sense of communal gathering, we introduced a great room at the base of the project to serve as a type of piazza for both the surrounding community and the bank. Its scale is civic. It also functions as an internal passage to the residential neighborhood to the north, and the apartments that form an important part of our complex. The bank's linkage to the context was intended to be programmatic as well as architectural.

The design of DZ Bank came six years after the design of 333 Wacker Drive in Chicago. With it my personal esthetic sensibility re-emerged as an intuitive force. For a short period of time I had gone through an unfruitful period exploring derivations of the classical language of architecture, as they applied to tall buildings. I was seeking to employ them to create the urban continuity between buildings found in the traditional city. I naively reasoned that such connections could be achieved in modern architecture—even with tall buildings. Of course, for this to happen, all architects needed to agree. After five years I acknowledged—collective agreement was not possible.

For me, the DZ Bank represented a new beginning, the idea that physical gesture is a fundamental strategy for bringing about connections in the modern city. I have used the strategy, with several variations, during the past 30 years. The buildings in this book seek to show the richness and variation of architectural gesture.

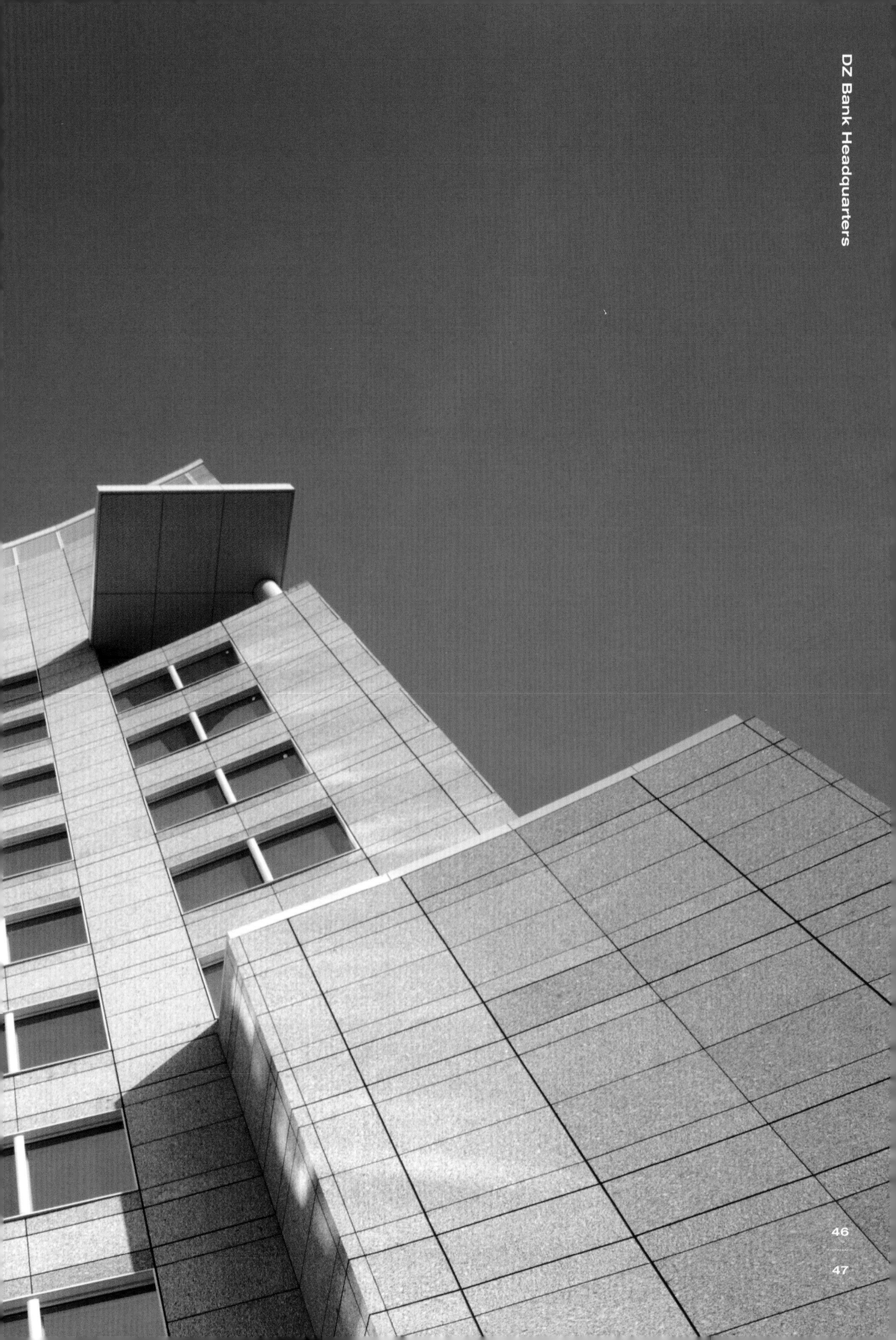

1250 René-Lévesque

Montréal, Québec, Canada — 1992

Context plan

Soon after the completion of the DZ Bank in Frankfurt we were commissioned by Marathon Realty to design the IBM Headquarters in Montreal. The site, known as 1250 René-Lévesque, is positioned on the southwest edge of the downtown core, directly opposite Montreal's imposing basilica, Mary Queen of the World.

In Montreal we elaborated the three-part, vertically striated composition of a tall building that we first explored in the DZ Bank. Rather than juxtaposing distinctly separate pieces of the tower, we interlocked a complex orthogonal geometry that we enhanced by interweaving stone and glass surface materials.

In Frankfurt, the German building code required close proximity to natural light for all office workers. However, in Montreal, North American regulations and the standards of the commercial real estate industry applied. Those dimensions tested whether our "fugal" composition of separate architectural parts was possible given the dimensional limitations. Our fugue, in fact, proved quite effective, especially in reducing the apparent bulk of a building of this type. Our first step after striating the building's mass vertically was to create interlocking, interpenetrating volumes that gestured to the context. We exploited this gestural strategy at every contextual opportunity.

Character and composition are two defining components of architecture. Like the human body, the tall building meets the ground, rises, and terminates in the air. This requires three distinct physical responses as a building works up through the pressures of different external influences. While the human body easily pivots and rotates reacting to lateral influences, a building's gestures are fixed. The external forces that affect a structure, such as adjacent pieces of the urban fabric, are also fixed and determined. The solar arc is predictable and a building's orientation can respond accordingly.

The most prominent, and closest, of the structures facing our site was the basilica. Our building's dominant visual element, a large curving glass façade, gestured to the basilica, acknowledging it. Facing predominately north, the façade had a minimal solar load. Opposite the ornate, rich stone texture of the church, our smooth, curving glass wall acted as a neutral backdrop. The east end of the façade flings itself out into space before returning to the wall of the tower, enclosing an intimate spatial overlook gesturing to the river beyond. The western end of the wall terminates with a vertical marker that supported an antenna which, extending to the building's highest point, became an architectural "planting of the flag." This civic marker on the skyline augmented, in Kevin Lynch's words, the city's "imageability." Equally important to the character of this curving wall was a lower volume thrusting through the façade 15 stories above the ground. The 11-story volume, which supports four cylindrical stainless steel columns, anchored itself to the plaza below and, at the height of the basilica's great dome, acknowledged its significance as an urban event. Farther up the façade, a great notch taken out of the curving glass wall revealed the upward movement of the building's central core—the third piece of our three part fugal composition. A large cantilevering cornice thrusting out into space terminated the high-rise, punctuating its place in the skyline.

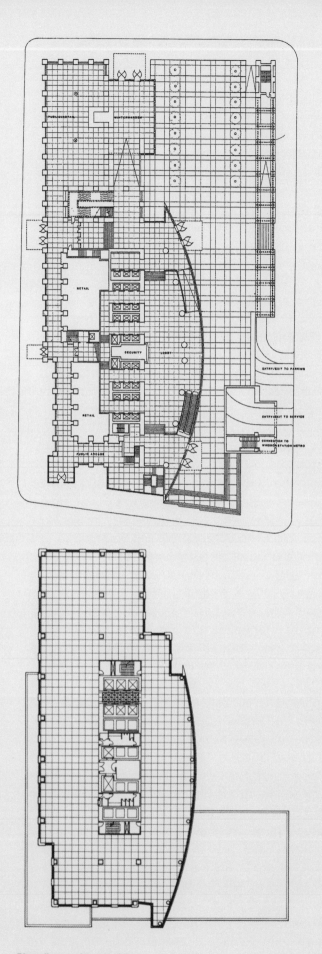

Plaza floor and tower plan

On the southwest elevation, the building's surface changed into a vertically striated series of cascading and interpenetrating slabs whose rich textures of stone and glass were calculated to reduce solar load. The slabs defined several key urban heights in the structure's rise from earth to sky. We initiated the stepped-back sequence with a four-story surface that holds and defines the street wall on Drummond. Each vertically succeeding plane receded 10 feet from the one below it until, at the top of the building, the wall surface stepped 40 feet back from the front edge of the building at the street.

The design of non-load-bearing curtain walls has been a preoccupation of architects since the beginning of the modern movement. Their quality has a profound influence on the perceived elegance of a tall building. Mies van der Rohe, for example, achieved a rare elegance in the Seagram Building in New York. Its main volume, a neutral box, was brought to life by a bronze clad structure of unsurpassed elegance. Our goal in tall buildings has been to combine animated volumetric urban gestures with surfaces that enhance the nobility and unity of their character. Because responding to different urban and solar conditions in Montreal led to different treatments on different façades, we employed various strategies to achieve overall cohesion—strategies that have become a signature for KPF. Personally, I think IBM's differentiated, responsive façade in Montreal is one of our most successful.

Twenty-five years after its completion, our design still stands as a model of logic based on an understanding of specific site conditions. Our design was not formalist but responsive: Montreal presented a particular environmental case. The degree of solar penetration through "vision glass" led us to different façades on the north and south. We have always been skeptical of double walls and metal shading louvers to reduce solar load because the embodied energy necessary to produce them is rarely compensated for over the life of a building, especially one at Montreal's latitude. We made a reduction of one-third of the vision surface from north to south by adding vertical granite surfaces five feet wide, which alternated with 10 feet of vision glass on the south, east, and west façades. Though a greater reduction in vision area is possible, marketing issues based on livability prevented further reduction. Floor to ceiling glass in the workplace has, because of user demand, come to define the accepted norm.

Although the two main façades differed markedly from each other, the design solution for each was based on the same process of weaving. In the predominately glass north-facing wall we introduced a major projecting horizontal stainless steel mullion midway between two opaque glass sections, which defined the floor and ceiling plenum construction. Between vision glass and opaque glass, additional minor stainless mullions were added. The visual strength of the projecting horizontals enhanced the reading of the curved surface, giving it a sense of being stretched taut. The all-glass wall meeting the intermittent stone verticals gave the appearance that each passed through the other. We wove the stone verticals with the stainless steel horizontals in a type of warp and weft.

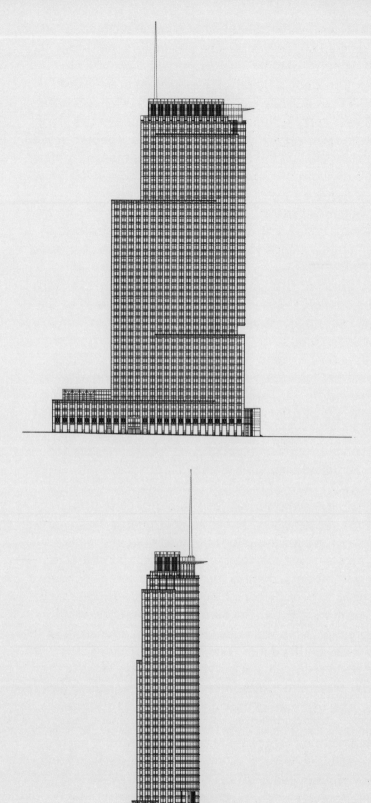

West and south elevations

As important as the building's presence in the sky is its presence at the street. We designed a winter garden and pergola and the entry plaza so that the building would play a welcoming civic role in Montreal's urban fabric. The footprint of this building is an L-shaped figure within the larger rectangular confines of the site's boundaries. Consequently, the northwest corner of the site is open for an exterior civic room facing the basilica and the Boulevard René-Lévesque— our main pedestrian approach. We implied visual enclosure for this exterior room by adding a low pergola facing Rue Stanley on the north. On its southern edge we introduced a large-scale winter garden, especially welcome given Montreal's climate. As a civic room, it has sponsored community events while also acting as a place for communal dining. For the building's main entry, we projected a curved volume two stories tall that followed the geometry of the north curving façade. The lower height gives a human scale to our exterior plaza as it weaves under the 11-story projecting wing of the office building on the east. The interaction and placement of these forms constitutes the most intense moment and exciting focus of the entire complex.

Within the entry lobby and winter garden we designed every aspect of the interior, creating bespoke lighting fixtures, reception desks, and elevators. Each of these reinforced the prevailing esthetic of the design. After many years, we were at last able to achieve a building that fully acknowledged the range of our intentions, from the city down to the detail.

Carwill House

Stratton, Vermont, U.S. — 1992

Site plan and elevation

In the late 1980s I met a retired corporate executive through a client with whom I had worked on a major project. He and his wife had purchased a steeply sloping site facing south toward Stratton Mountain in Vermont. They asked me to recommend an architect. I recommended myself.

Residential architecture was a new adventure for me. Most architects begin their careers designing houses, but I started with large-scale commercial projects. I was eager to work small.

Working on a home is intensely personal, and freighted with responsibility. An architect has to develop a sympathetic understanding of the clients' hopes and aspirations, especially because making a home around a family and marriage marks an important stage for the clients: the experience can bring much pleasure if the relationship between architect and clients is mutually respectful and supportive. Here again, my "comparative process" assisted in giving us common ground so that we could work together as a "we."

The narrowness of the site and neighboring structures on both sides discouraged extending the house from east to west to face the dramatic view of Stratton Mountain broadside. Instead we followed the north-south orientation down the steepest part of the terrain.

This orientation also allowed, while entering the site, an unimpeded view of the mountain, making it possible to frame the view both from the site and within the house. My aspiration, then, was to heighten the drama of the view starting with the approach by structuring oblique gestures in the landscape. On the east, by taking a north-south slice out of the top of the rocky slope, we created a framing wall on what would become the entry court. This linear slice revealed the profile of the rocky terrain (and shielded the entry court from the easterly neighbor), and it dramatically pointed toward the view of the mountain. We then anchored the site's southern end with an outdoor fireplace.

To counterbalance what was emerging as a strong north-south axis, we composed a series of obliquely intersecting volumes and planes, and then organized them to pivot around a cylindrical entry tower topped by a study with an eagle-eye view of the Vermont mountains.

My clients anticipated frequent family visits. For privacy, we took advantage of the downward, south-facing slope and positioned the master bedroom one story below the main living spaces and the guest bedrooms a story above. The grotto-like location for the master bedroom gave it a sense of intimacy and seclusion, a feeling that we enhanced by bringing stonewalls from the exterior into the room, where we designed hand-crafted, built-in wooden furniture. A projecting stair tower, on the western side of the house, leads to the guest bedrooms while offering another view of Stratton Mountain.

Our clients wanted a grand but informal and intimate room that combined both living and dining. This heart-space of the house, especially because of the height, required careful attention to composition, detail, and the handling of natural light. The shape of this room was critical. To contrast with the angularity of the

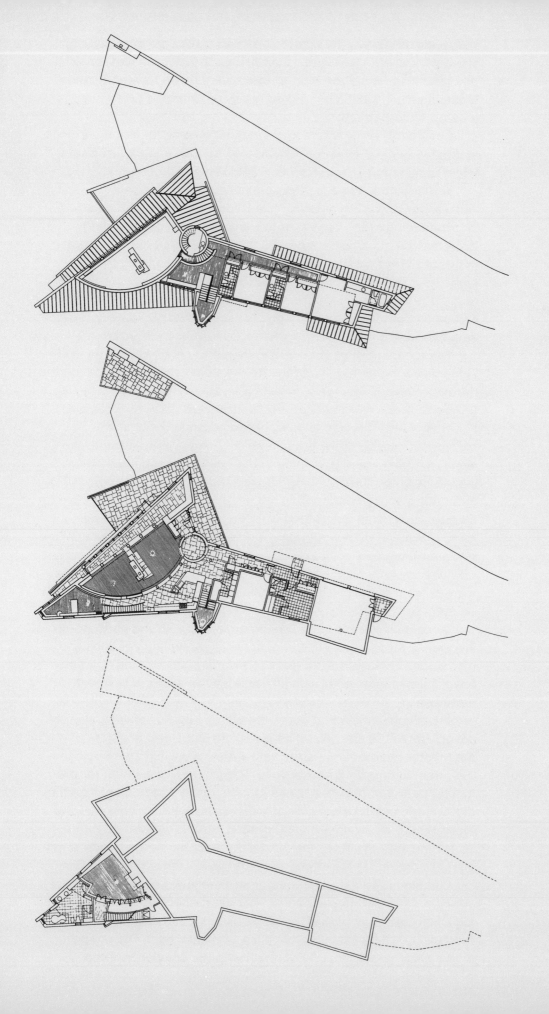

volumes surrounding this room, we designed a dominant curving side. For different light sources for different times of the day, we drew light in high on one side of the room, and low on the other. Within the curving wall, we placed clerestory windows configured in a two-step profile, and within the clerestory, we designed the light itself by placing closely spaced vertical fins so that the sun projects separate lines streaking across the surfaces of the room. To create intimacy, we positioned single-story spaces that surrounded and opened onto the tall space. An open kitchen, with a bar-like serving counter, faces the living-dining room on one side, and on another side, a low intimate sitting area faces in. Its external wall is entirely glazed, bringing light low into the main room. Within this space a massive stone fireplace reaches the sloping ceiling, dividing the living from the dining area, contributing powerfully to the character of this mountain house. The long curve of the dominant wall recalls the curves of the cylindrical entry and the projecting tower, effectively forming a cluster that contrasts dramatically with the oblique volumes of the rest of the house.

We knew from the beginning of the project that the ruggedness of the site would inspire rugged materials, but those materials had to agree with the design as it evolved. After considering many alternatives, we selected rough-sawn cedar planks, one-foot wide and eight-feet long to clad and modulate the façades. We separated each plank with reveals and anchored each end with exposed stainless steel bolts, which shine when struck by the sun, contrasting with the wood. For exterior paving we chose a blue/gray slate to relate to the natural stone of the site, and cut it into thick cubic pieces that we randomly placed so that the house appears to grow organically out of the rock within which it is embedded. For the roofs and for several curved and faceted exterior surfaces, we chose lead-coated copper, which would patina with age.

Designing houses can often be a stimulus and a laboratory for formal investigation with an application to buildings of larger scale. It certainly was for me. About the time of this design I also worked on the IBM Headquarters and Gannett/USA TODAY Headquarters. Much of the visual sensibility that emerged in those two buildings had its beginning in this house. Working at all scales is vitally important for an architect. There is nothing more dispiriting than to be typecast as an architect specializing in a single building type, and nothing more enjoyable than working with every type at every scale.

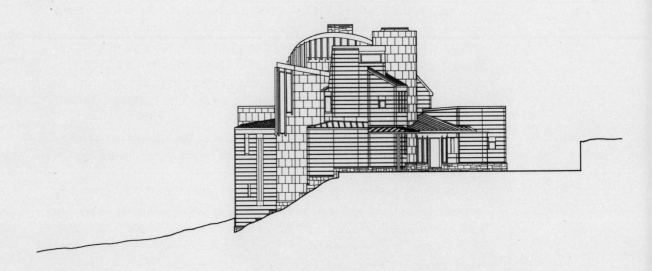

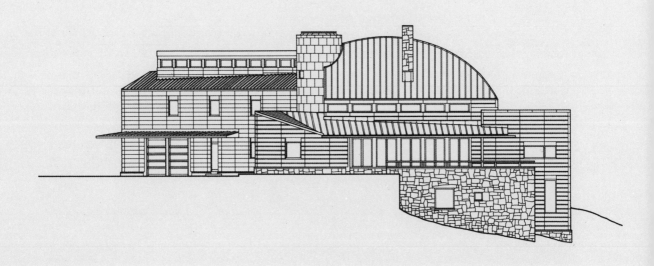

North and west elevation
Opposite: section through living and dining room

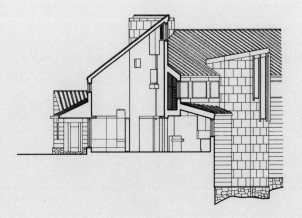

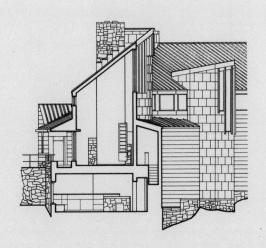

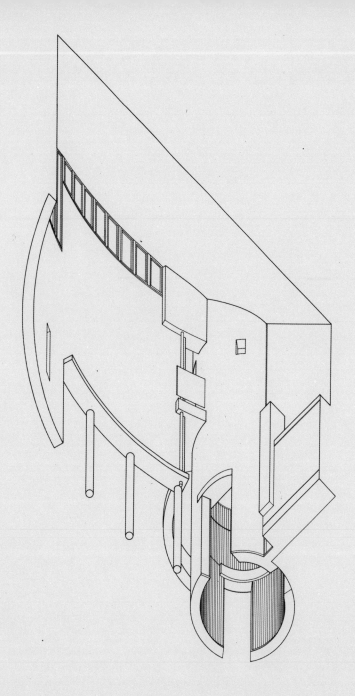

"Worm's eye" axonometric of living / dinning room

Federal Reserve
Bank of Dallas

Dallas, Texas, U.S. – 1992

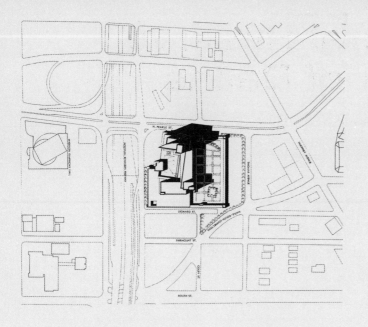

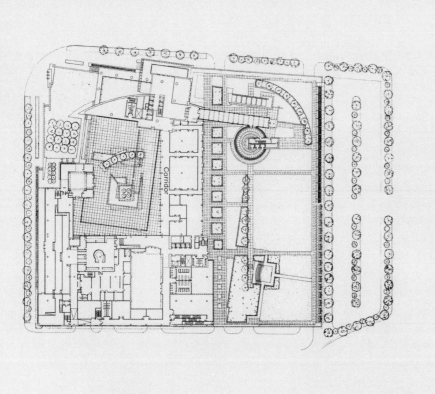

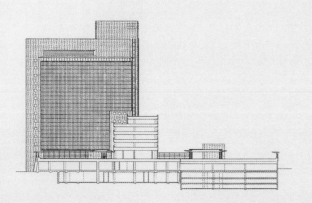

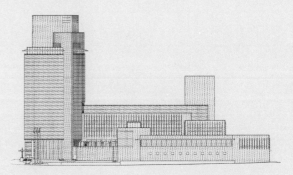

Site plan, garden floor plan, longitudinal section, and south elevation

The Dallas Federal Reserve Bank was the first of four major buildings I designed for the United States Federal Government. Balancing security, accessibility, openness, and a sense of timeless permanence was a primary goal in all the projects, but in the Federal Reserve we especially strived to capture, through architecture, the dignity and strength of this unique institution. Our challenge was to express a sense of both serenity and welcome without resorting to outdated visual clichés such as colonnaded monumentality.

The site was an eight-acre parcel on the northern side of the Woodhull Rogers Freeway, a circumferential artery that surrounds Dallas's downtown core. By coincidence, our most immediate neighbor to the south of the freeway across from our site was The Morton H. Meyerson Symphony Center, designed by my mentor I.M. Pei. Other than I.M.'s hall and the city itself, little existed around our site that could elicit an architectural gesture. Later, after we designed the building, a section of the freeway to the west of our site was decked over, creating a welcoming civic bridge between downtown and the residential neighborhoods to the north.

The Reserve Bank needed two levels of security. We housed the areas requiring the higher level in a fortified podium on the building's lowest floors, which enclosed a maze of corridors, bullet-proof rooms, a shooting range, three large loading docks, and several mechanized vaults. Natural light was not required, or desired. Additionally, we extended the podium with a decked parking structure that matched its height, bringing the parking north to fill out the site. The decked parking paired with the podium to effectively create a raised landform that supported the greater portion of the building's program in the structure above.

On this constructed landform we built two separate garden courtyards, each with a distinct character. At the outer edge of the decked parking we contained the northern garden with a pergola. Within this garden we created a circular enclosed glass structure that served as an entry pavilion from the parking decks below. To encourage social gathering, we encircled the south courtyard, over the podium, with all of the active elements of the building's program. Dining areas, employee lounges, a health club facility, beauty and barber shops, training facilities, and an auditorium all opened onto this elevated town square, which became the social heart of the whole building.

Above, multiple levels of office space for various departments surrounded the square. The different programmatic requirements allowed us to mass the building above the landform into a staggered silhouette of volumes that spiraled up from, and around, the square. Step by step, the overall dimensions of the floors decreased. Starting at the base with the largest of the levels, a C-shaped floor plan transformed into an L-shaped floor above, and then into the tower itself. A pivoting, tower-like volume containing vertical circulation punctuated the joint between the separate arms of the office floor plates, and became a physical marker in the vertical ascent. From high to low, this cascading, spinning massing embraced the garden room below without surrounding it completely.

A large physical separation between the tower and the dining pavilion opened to the Meyerson, singling it out in the cityscape and establishing an urban relationship. The benefits of the opening were multiple. It offered an ideal exposure to the southern sun, and established a deferential relationship that honors the Meyerson. The relationship between the two buildings opened a visual conversation that we enhanced by cladding our building in limestone that matched the Meyerson. Each building also related to the other geometrically by sharing an angular inflection of the site. We responded to the inflection point by rotating the positions of our tower and the glazed entry below, a gesture that animated the composition of the main volumes of our building. Through scale, materials, and gesture, we linked the two structures into an architectural community: the buildings talked to each other.

A weaving of horizontal and vertical textures characterizes the structure's overall composition. Horizontal striation typifies large surfaces of glass, while a vertical striation dominates the limestone surfaces, even when they are fenestrated. Closely spaced limestone mullions, capped with painted metal fins, enhance this vertical reading. The woven interplay of horizontal and vertical volumes and textures culminates in our most dramatic gesture, the curved limestone prow that slices through the body of the tower. A backdrop to the fully glazed volume of the tower, the prow anchors the rising masses of the building. A strong vertical urban marker, the prow gestures to the freeway, the city, and the Meyerson as it punctuates the skyline and declares the presence of the Dallas Federal Reserve Bank in the city.

First Hawaiian Bank Headquarters

Honolulu, Hawaii, U.S. – 1995

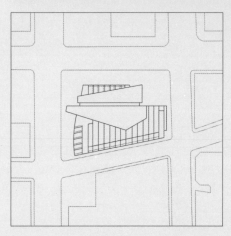

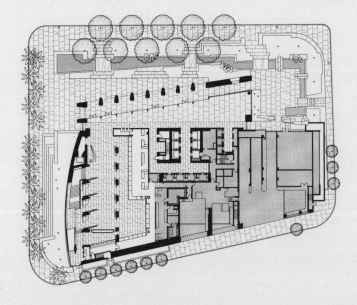

Context, site, and ground-floor plan

To express a Hawaiian sense of place in the design of the First Hawaiian Bank in Honolulu, we intended to mediate—and dramatize—the verticality of the nearby mountains and the horizontality of the sea by engaging the urban landscape. In this case what architects often metaphorically call the "urban landscape" was literal, given the mountains and sea embracing the city.

But in addition to a contextually responsive design, I wanted to capture a sense of Hawaiian character. To me, a Minnesotan by birth, Hawaii means warmth—not just the balmy climate but also the warmth of the hospitality. Hawaii is inviting. Through a composition that embodied the character of the island, the building could be the same.

Our client, Walter Dods, the bank's CEO and Chairman, recognized that in order to make the building inviting, it needed a space dedicated to welcoming the community. Consequently, he brought the Hawaii Museum of Contemporary Art into the project and placed it directly within the main banking hall. Unusual for a bank, the program of a museum was an ideal welcoming gesture.

Arranging for a banking hall and a museum to share space at the base of a tower, however, necessitated compositional and dimensional sensitivity, which involved the invention of a new high-rise configuration. A horizontal base of several stories supporting a tower would prevent the vertical structure from growing from the earth, but the problem could be corrected if the tower interlocked with the lower structure in a complex relationship. To break the impasse, we brought a portion of the tower, the visually weightier part, directly to the earth.

In the two previous tall buildings represented in this book, Frankfurt and Montreal, we utilized what I called a "fugal" composition of three architectural voices interlocking together. Here, because we wanted to heighten the drama of the mountain and sea conditions, we elected to express the relationship of only two prime architectural voices. By creating a horizontal interlocking base, we actually introduced a third architectural voice, but the dominant impression was the interplay of the horizontal and the vertical, the mountains and the sea.

It is usually more efficient to position elevators in the center of a tower. But in Honolulu, because elevators placed outside a building do not figure as part of the zoning area, the code encouraged us to locate the tower's vertical circulation on the perimeter. Liberating elevators from the bowels of the building allowed visitors to experience vertical movement from within glass elevators, while looking out at the surroundings. This placement initiated the configuration of the tower's floor plate.

We invoked the mountains and sea in other ways. Because mountains are perceived as heavy, and the ocean, which reflects the sky, is perceived as light, we combined a visually weighty part with a visually buoyant section. Facing the mountains, the weighty part is composed of vertically striated stone bracketing vision glass, rising straight from earth to sky. The buoyant part, facing the sea, is horizontally striated, with alternating bands of opaque and vision glass. Mountains rise, the sea extends, and the corresponding parts of this building do the same.

The design of speculative commercial office buildings usually requires rectangular floor plates with a generous dimension from the core to the outside wall. The speculative nature of the commission encourages generic rather than custom, geometrically complex floor plates. The First Hawaiian Bank, however, was a corporate headquarters, and much to our delight, our client wanted to give the office floor plate an abundance of unique conditions that could be exploited to generate greater spatial intimacy and variety.

Our site was trapezoidal, with a diagonal side that determined the shape of a parallelogram. The boundaries of the site are essentially defined by the building's base on two of its sides. On the other two, the more public faces, we brought the main façades back from Kirby and Bishop Streets to create a landscaped setback, which we planted with tropical vegetation and embellished with artwork. These two façades act as a prelude to entering the museum and main banking hall. The tower's north façade, facing Kirby Street, addresses the mountains, and rises cliff-like from ground to roof. This angled wall initiates the wedge-shaped geometry that determines the tower's plan.

The unique faceting on each face of the tower responds directly to the urban orientation it addresses. The broad south face folds out to give better views of the sea. The exposed elevators, inserted at the fold, energize the façade with their movement. On the west face along Bishop, the tower's two main parts meet dramatically: at their most slender, the two parts pair to create a vertical energy that is accentuated by the outwardly leaning prow of the glass volume. The west face is the building's most emphatic urban marker.

Also along Bishop Street, at grade, a bespoke curving façade of cast-glass brings natural light into the museum space. Designed by the architect-artist James Carpenter, it refracts light into its prismatic spectral components, bathing the interior space in its continually changing qualities. A grand staircase behind the cast-glass wall ascends to the mezzanine of the museum, its sculptural variations and light refractions exercising a magnetic attraction to museum visitors that lures them up to the mezzanine.

Imparting a character of place to our designs has always been an objective, especially given the leveling influences of globalism. Buildings must speak specifically about their place and time. To make the building feel Hawaiian, we selected a warm palette of materials. The coloration of the limestone resembles the color of Hawaii's sandy beaches. The reflective quality and coloration of the glass echoes that of the sea and the sky. Craft is also evident in the delicacy of internal wooden screens, which filter and dapple natural light, and in the cast glass wall of the Bishop Street façade, which captures the light quality of Hawaii's solar latitude. The landscaping, a balanced combination of water, stone, and vegetation, contributes to the building's Hawaiian character.

Yet this this is done without overtly evoking any period from Hawaii's past. Entirely of its time, it doesn't try to look "Hawaiian." It tries to be "Hawaiian."

The World Bank
Headquarters

Washington, DC, U.S. — 1996

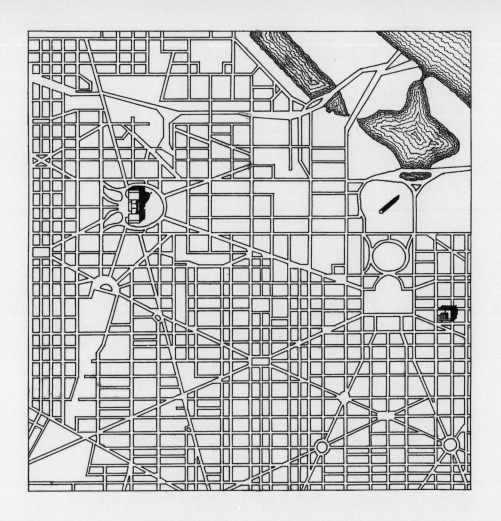

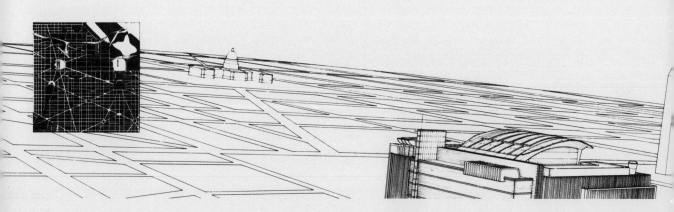

Context plan

In 1989 we were invited to participate in an international competition for the re-design of The World Bank Headquarters on Pennsylvania Avenue in Washington, D.C. Their then-existing complex consisted of six buildings incoherently assembled on a full city block. The impediment this created to the functioning and the spirit of the Bank was exacerbated by insufficient space, which was enough to house less than half its staff. At the time the bank had 12,000 employees, the majority of whom were housed in various buildings in the surrounding neighborhood.

Assuming that all the existing buildings would be replaced, the competition anticipated a phased construction process over ten years. Two of the buildings, one designed by Gordon Bunshaft of SOM and the other by Vincent Kling, had been built less than thirty years before. While neither was a distinguished piece of architecture, we found they could be resuscitated if architecturally modified. Of the eight international competitors, we were the only architects to make this recommendation. Our suggestion, which would eventually save the bank 100 million dollars and years of delay in the full build-out, gave us an advantage in the competition. Of the 2,100,000 sq.ft. in the final structure, a full 40 percent of this area was within the two original buildings.

A second convincing suggestion was to provide 13 stories within the 130-foot height limitation allowed by D.C. zoning. Most commercial buildings in the capital allowed only 12 floors, given standard floor-to-floor working height, and all our competitors made this assumption. We discovered, however, that if we could reduce the structure and plenum depth by using an efficient post-tensioned flat slab construction, providing under floor ductwork traveling very short distances, we could reduce the floor-to-floor height to 10 feet. The resulting efficiency accommodated 13 floors within the zoning height limitation. Adding the 13th floor enabled us to create more building perimeter area for private offices facing natural light and to provide more open space within the complex.

Why were these environmental qualities important? The World Bank recruits highly qualified personnel from around the globe, most of them well established in their field. Their environment matters to them, and they prefer private offices and want access to natural light. Providing natural light to the required number of private offices is a product of the linear perimeter of the structure. Not only did we increase the exterior perimeter surface of the building because of the additional floor, but we also found that by introducing an interior atrium covered by a curved glass skylight, offices facing an inner courtyard could receive natural light with the additional advantage that they faced the vibrant activity it attracted and stimulated.

Achieving privacy within the courtyard so that offices didn't face each other at close range required a space of generous dimensions. We began by positioning a cubic room, 150'×150'×150', in the center of the site. (D.C. zoning allowed visual embellishments such as skylights to rise above the zoning limit of 130'.) We pinwheeled four distinct volumes of workspace around this room. The existing L-shaped relationship of the SOM building and the Kling building

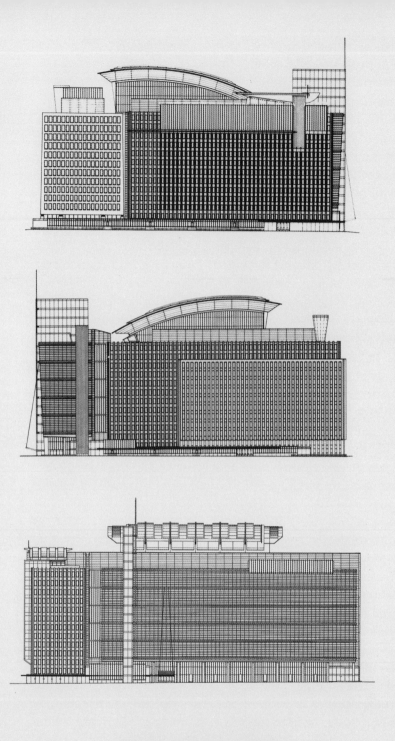

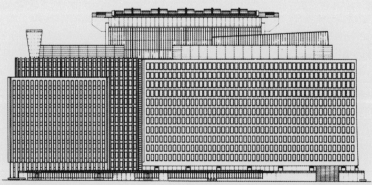

Top to bottom: east, west, north and south elevations

initiated the pinwheel, and we added two more volumes of workspace of similar dimensions to complete a four-unit composition turning around the courtyard. The dimensions of this generous interior space precluded any office looking directly into another opposite. The courtyard-facing offices ended up being the preferred spaces.

But the spatial success of a large skylit interior room was hardly guaranteed. Without human-scale elements providing activity and intimacy, an interior court can seem vacuous and lifeless. We searched for programs that would bring people together and help fulfill the social mission of the space.

First, we broke up the huge space by introducing five cylindrical columns, each five feet in diameter, that rise to within 15 feet of the curving skylight, where they branch into a pyramidal cluster of steel arms that support the ribs of the skylight. We built a ground plane of several different levels around the columns, to create more intimate zones. The main level opens down to the dining functions below within a large trapezoidal void of space punctuated by the tall columns. A column of water, spilling down from the main level, transforms this lowest level into a reflecting pool that faces the cafeteria and private dining areas. The pool is animated by surface effects in the water created by natural light striking it from the skylight above. The main level also steps up, forming a series of terraces that encourage informal gathering and provide seating for large events.

We also positioned several elements within the main courtyard that become rooms within the room. A vertical stack of enclosed conference areas formed a tower-like structure on the north side of the space. A curving platform low in the space, accessed by a staircase, engaged the great columns. Seating adjacent to a café established an intimate area below this viewing platform. Along the eastern side of the room a series of free-standing vertical elements provided surfaces for changing art exhibitions, and they engaged a linear water course spilling down to the floor below. Tall pyramidal skylights giving human scale to the court brought light down to the cafeteria.

The courtyard has attracted an extraordinary number of events of different types. Though a single individual feels comfortable being totally alone in the space, it can also host hundreds of people for dinners, lectures, and spontaneous gatherings. It is an architectural void, but an actively occupied void that has become the living heart of the institution.

But it was the highly efficient planning of the new working spaces forming half the perimeter of the great room that made the concept of the building possible. Our two new office blocks each have a linear spine of services bisecting their length. We positioned continuous chases for vertical ducting on either side of these spines, which enabled exceedingly shallow horizontal air ducts. A 30'×30' structural column bay made the thin, nine-inch, post-tensioned, uplit concrete slab possible, which we left exposed in the offices.

To mark the entry within the full-block mass, we lifted one of our two additions, the north-facing bar looking to Pennsylvania

116
—
117

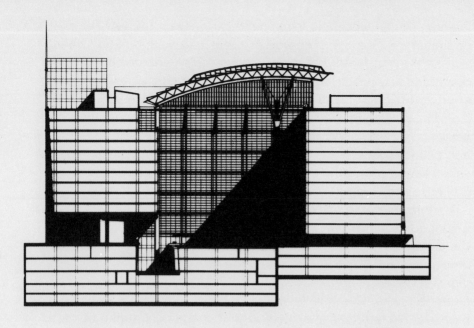

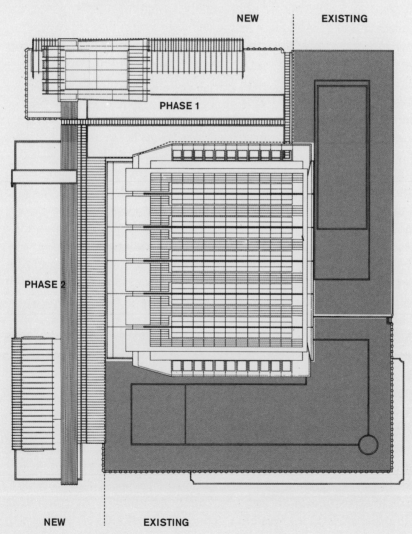

NEW   EXISTING

PHASE 1

PHASE 2

NEW   EXISTING

Atrium section, phasing plan

Avenue, off the ground to create a three-story entry lobby that would house an exhibition on The World Bank's history. Lifting the mass and opening the façade was a gesture of welcome, one that we dramatized by canting the glass façade overhead.

But retaining two of the existing buildings and visually integrating them into the external expression of the building posed a question. They could either be entirely re-clad or they could be integrated, as is, into the new composite structure. We chose the latter. Both buildings had a similar external expression—vertical precast concrete elements. Using this as a point of departure, we strove to integrate the complex into a unified whole at a higher aesthetic pitch that still respected the existing context and history. Our aspiration to create contextual linkage is one of our distinguishing characteristics as architects.

This weave of the old and new created a visual collage that transformed the urban expression of The World Bank. Our new north façade on Pennsylvania Avenue, entirely clad in glass, had a strong horizontal expression. We wove closely-spaced mullions through the vertical striations of the precast concrete elements, creating a type of warp and weft that tied all the building's multiple components together into a unified whole. A powerful vertical volume marking the building's entry anchored the entire composition.

Two other significant forms positioned high in the building joined the enormous convex curvature of the atrium's skylight. One enclosed the main boardroom and the second, the ceremonial conference room. Together they animated the building's upper profile addressing Pennsylvania Avenue. Entered from the uppermost floor of the building, the rooms could break the 130' height limit since the zoning authorities viewed them as ornamental spaces that were honorific. Natural light enters each of these sculptural forms in a dramatic but different manner. The boardroom's comes from a high curving clerestory. Light for the ceremonial conference room enters through a large north-facing projecting glass tube of space. We dressed each of the rooms in fittingly elegant materials and furnished them with our own custom-designed pieces.

The World Bank allowed us to craft every aspect of the building's design. The biology of its structural and mechanical systems enabled its form. Its form enabled the material and volumetric interplay of its exterior and interior surfaces. This interplay inspired the character and design of its furnishings. Given a supportive client keen on building a good architectural citizen in the nation's capital, the commission allowed us to design at large scale a gesamtkunstwerk that expressed the character of this uniquely important institution.

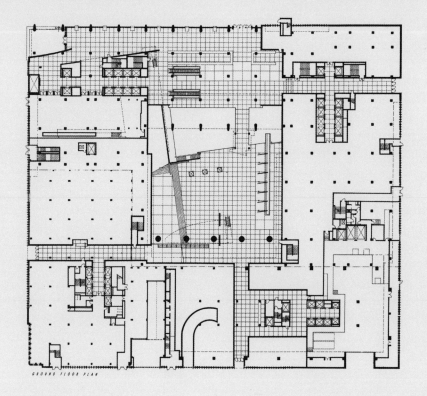

GROUND FLOOR PLAN

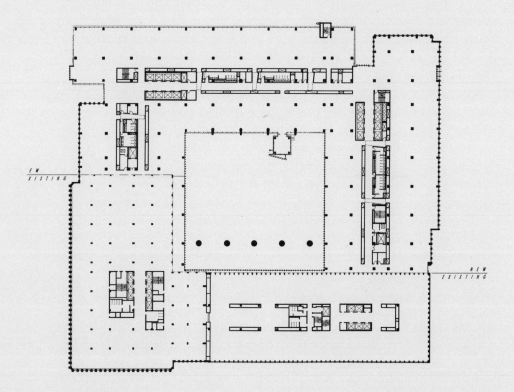

NEW
EXISTING

NEW
EXISTING

Atrium floor plan, typical floor plan

U.S. Courthouse Portland

Portland, Oregon, U.S. – 1997

Context plan

The words inscribed on the wall of the Portland Federal Courthouse—
"The First Duty of Society is Justice"—established from the outset
our architectural mission: to say the same in the form of architecture.
In three buildings we designed for the U.S. federal court system,
I strived to represent the meaning of the words architecturally,
starting with our first, The Mark O. Hatfield Federal Courthouse in
Portland, Oregon, completed in 1994 under the General Service
Administration's new Design Excellence program.

Fundamentally, the typology of courthouses is composed of two
parts: the courtrooms and the office spaces that serve the courts.
The measured, honorific design of the courtrooms where justice
is balanced is in some way poetic, while the design of the offices
that serve the courtrooms is prosaic. In federal courthouses, the
architecture should embody the poetry and prose underlying the
judicious application of the law.

The judicial realm is composed of three fundamental zones.
Each requires a separate bank of elevators. Public circulation to the
courtrooms is the first of these banks. Departing from the building's
entry lobby, elevators bring visitors to a generous gallery on each
courtroom floor. Judges and their staff taking elevators to their
chambers and courtrooms use a second bank of elevators, which
is entered from secure parking on the lowest level of the building.
A third bank, transporting defendants, requires the highest level of
security. This bank ascends from the U.S. Marshall's facility directly
under the stack of courtrooms and brings defendants into a holding
area between a pair of courtrooms where they remain until they enter
the courtroom. Since the holding area serves two courtrooms, all U.S.
federal courthouses are designed in paired courtrooms. The number
of pairs depends on the horizontal dimension of the site. Our site
was relatively small, only 200 feet in width, so each of our floors has
only two courtrooms.

The three separate elevator banks generate a basic courtroom
floor with three separate functional zones of different spatial type.
The first zone provides entry to the courtroom for the public and
the lawyers representing defendants. We designed this zone to be
open, spatially generous, and welcoming, and to provide entry to the
courtrooms as well as a release from them. Courtrooms are highly
stressful, and we wanted these spaces to offer an emotional escape
from the deliberations inside. We designed these entry spaces to
provide natural light and to offer views of the surrounding city. Seen
from the exterior, they represent an open and transparent judicial
process.

The courtrooms themselves, their holding areas, and jury
deliberation rooms constitute the second zone. A judge's ability to
efficiently process cases is greatly affected by the design of the
courtroom, so we spent considerable effort insuring the proper
relationship of the parts. Once that relationship was achieved, we
focused on the emotional effect the courtroom produces, striving for
warmth, humanity, dignity, and serenity.

Without natural light, the objective would be impossible, but how
do you introduce natural light into a room with no external exposure?

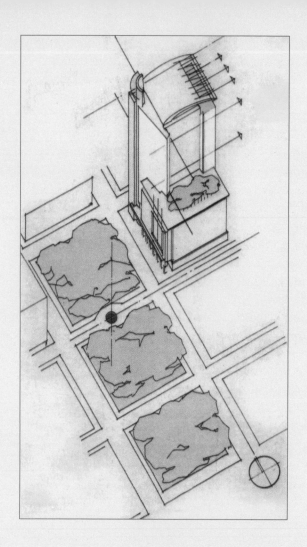

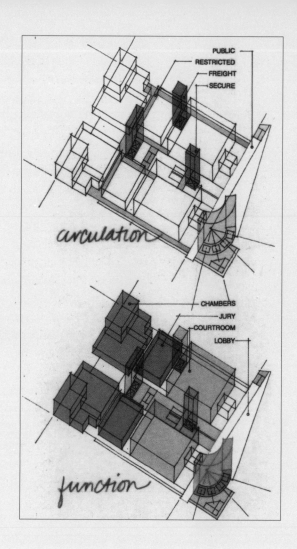

circulation

function

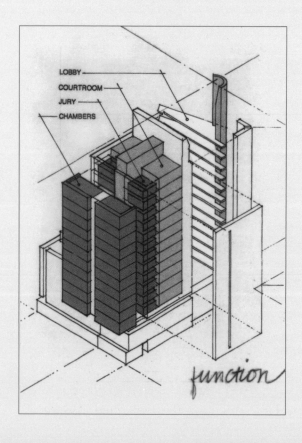

LOBBY

COURTROOM

JURY

CHAMBERS

function

We found the answer above the ceilings. Because the 18' mandated height of courtrooms in the U.S. federal system must be maintained throughout the entire floor, the space between the ceiling slab and the lower ceiling of the holding areas can accommodate building services, and the same spaces over the corridors along the sides of the building can serve as clerestory spaces that channel natural light into the courtrooms directly over the jury boxes. Coming from the side over the jury, the light causes no glare for either the jury or the judge but, illuminating the wood paneling, it creates a warm and dignified atmosphere.

The third zone was the judges' chambers. Two courtrooms on a floor required two judges' chambers, each positioned directly behind its courtroom, along with the jury deliberation room. A judge and a jury need take only a few steps from the bench or the jury box to chambers or the deliberation room.

Unlike the design of tall commercial buildings, a Federal Courthouse has a very specific program that exerts pressures on a building from the inside that largely shape the building. However, the external context also exerts pressures on its form that must be acknowledged if the building is to participate meaningfully in its context.

Portland's city plan is gridded in blocks 200 feet square, dimensions that contribute to the city's intimate urban character. The courthouse site occupied a full block, and to the west, a wooded park three-blocks long provided a generous foreground in the heart of the city that would set off the building's civic importance. We positioned the main feature of our building, a limestone-clad elevator tower, in the park's line of sight.

The building's main feature is a limestone-clad tower enclosing the public vertical circulation to the courtrooms. Four elevators, arrayed in a crescent shape, form the inner core of this tower, and a stair wraps around this core, which rises to a crown at its apex that fans out to the city below.

Anyone attending court steps off the elevator into a long, linear, tapering gallery with courtrooms on one side and the city on the other. The walls outside the courtrooms are paneled in wood, its entry doors clad in leather, while the walls facing the city are entirely glazed and shaded with horizontal projections. This glass wall angles toward the park, as though acknowledging it. A glass-enclosed stair at the far end of the gallery, cantilevered out into space, terminates the room. Its dramatic position draws visitors, encouraging use.

From the park, the building introduces itself in segmented blocks, the lower block scaled to the pedestrian on the street, and the upper to the city and skyline. A low seven-floor volume enclosing the agencies that support the court roomn faces the park, forming an architectural billboard articulated in stone, glass, and steel. Faced in limestone, framing a powerful square of glass, the façade supports three vertical pylons that hold flagpoles signaling the courthouse's civic role.

This limestone façade, lifted off the body of the building on shadowy reveals, addresses the street. Behind and above it, the

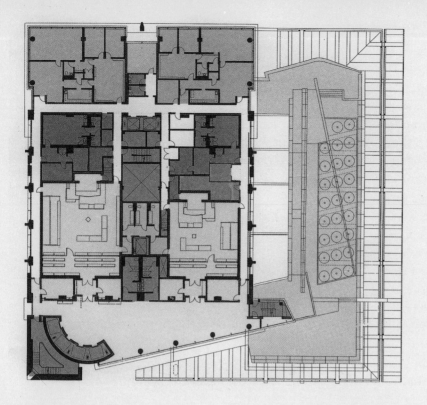

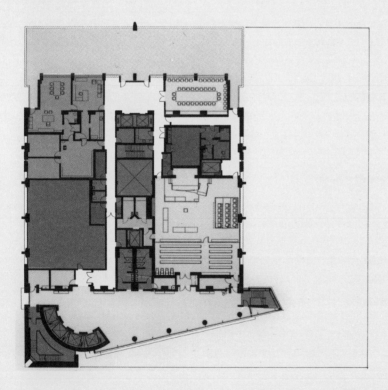

Typical courts floor plan

courtrooms, the holding rooms, and the jury deliberation spaces occupy a second volume, bracketed on each side by façades clad in limestone. Apertures for the natural light that enters the courtrooms from these two sides striate the façade, set deeply into its walls. The apparent depth, as though carved from solid stone, reinforces the courtrooms' sense of solidity and security, and the building's—and institution's—stability. The glazed public galleries lie to one side of this zone, and the judges' chambers, also glazed, to the other. At each floor level the glass volumes are strapped onto the adjacent limestone façades with strongly expressed metal bands.

At the top of the 11-story stack of courtrooms, naturalization ceremonies and other gatherings are held in a vaulted room that steps back from the façades below. A terrace facing east to Mount Hood accommodates receptions after naturalization ceremonies and other events.

Our goal was to design a U.S. Federal Courthouse that explained its function visually. Instead of boxing all functions in a simple, singular enclosure that masked functions within a single geometry, we expressed the working functions of the courthouse by massing the zones in separate blocks. We hope that the greater legibility helps explain the inner workings of providing justice—"The First Duty of Society"— even before reading the words on the wall.

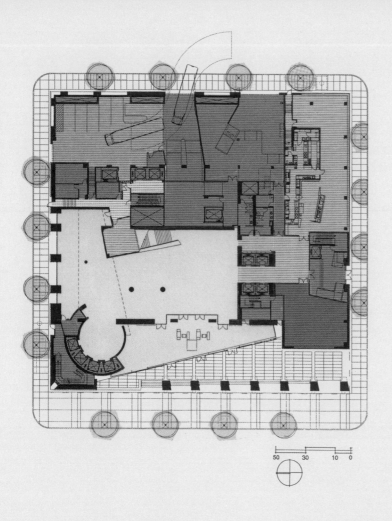

50 30 10 0

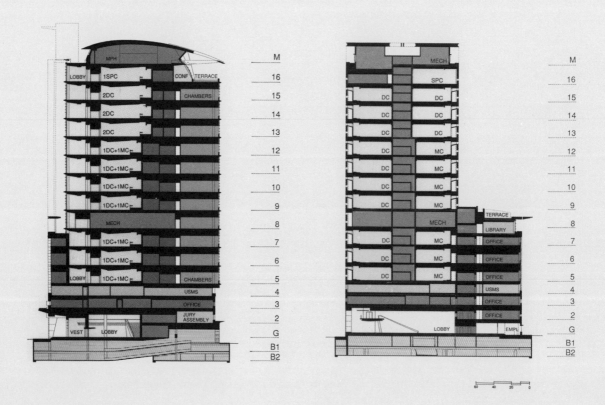

		M
MPH		
LOBBY	1SPC	CONF TERRACE
	2DC	CHAMBERS
	2DC	
	2DC	
	1DC+1MC	
	1DC+1MC	
	1DC+1MC	
	1DC+1MC	
	MECH	
	1DC+1MC	
	1DC+1MC	
LOBBY	1DC+1MC	CHAMBERS
		USMS
		OFFICE
		JURY ASSEMBLY
VEST	LOBBY	

M
16
15
14
13
12
11
10
9
8
7
6
5
4
3
2
G
B1
B2

			M
	MECH		
		SPC	
DC	DC		
DC	DC		
DC	DC		
DC	MC		
DC	MC		
DC	MC		
DC	MC		
MECH		TERRACE	
DC	MC	LIBRARY	
DC	MC	OFFICE	
DC	MC	OFFICE	
DC	MC	OFFICE	
		USMS	
		OFFICE	
		OFFICE	
LOBBY		EMPL	

M
16
15
14
13
12
11
10
9
8
7
6
5
4
3
2
G
B1
B2

60 40 20 0

Ground floor plan and sections

THE FIRST DUTY OF SOCIETY

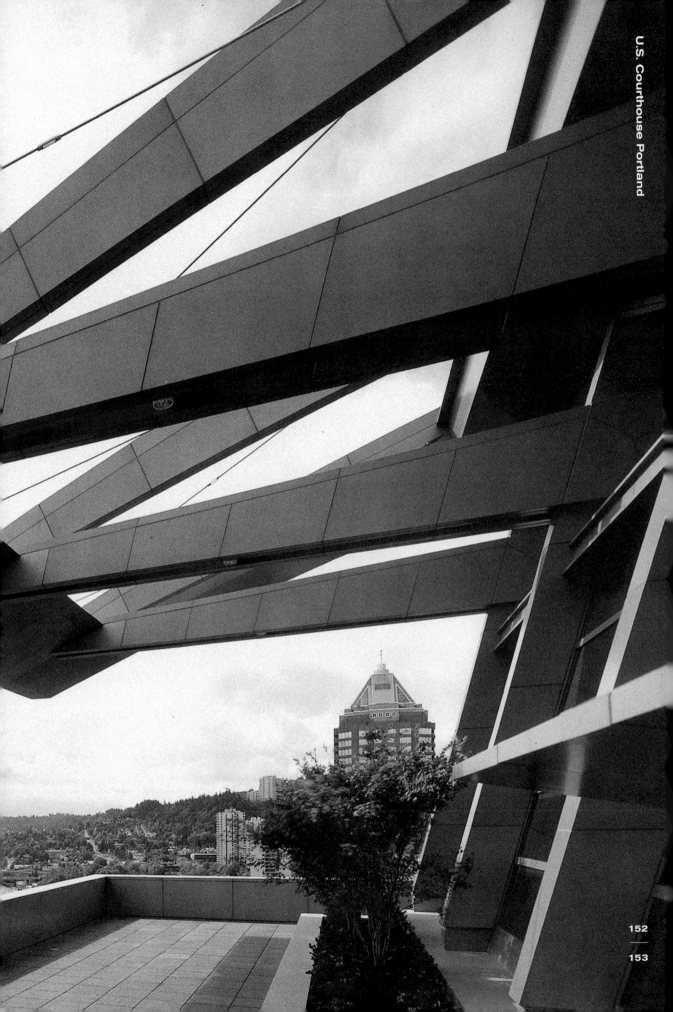

IBM World Headquarters

Armonk, New York, U.S. – 1997

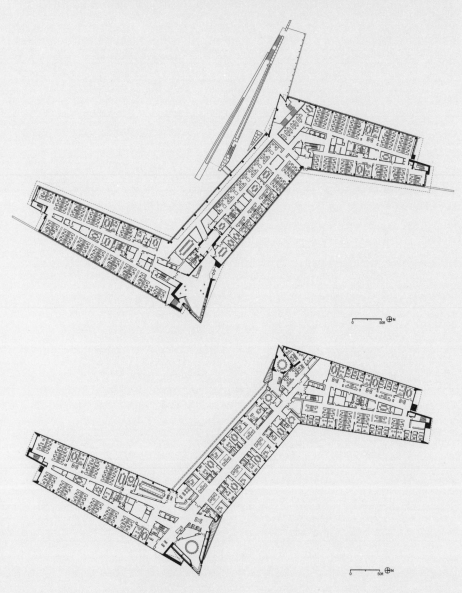

Context, and first and second-floor plan

When he became chairman of IBM in 1993, Louis Gerstner was charged with the mission of turning the huge corporate ocean liner around, and when he hired us, it was to enlist architecture as an instrument to engineer the turnaround. For IBM's new headquarters in Armonk, New York, he had a clear idea of the direction the architecture should take, despite his own architectural instincts: "If I were building this for myself, it would look like Brideshead revisited. But, I'm not: it needs to look, and function, like the technology we're known for."

When we started designing, IBM's headquarters was located about a mile from the future site in a '60s building by SOM, designed at a time of IBM's market dominance. By the '80s their dominance had waned, and much was changing in their corporate structure. Brought in to transform the company, Mr. Gerstner deployed architecture to help him establish a new workplace ethic in a structure that would be leaner, smaller, and more agile than the '60s headquarters it was replacing. Mr. Gerstner wanted to position himself in the middle of the action, not in a remote corner, where he could see, and be seen by, his teams.

In contrast to their original site, a broad open expanse of relatively flat terrain, this new 450-acre property, densely wooded with oak, was steeply contoured with rocky outcroppings. Within Armonk's zoning, which limited the structure's height to three stories, we wanted the building to engage nature in a complementary yin-yang relationship that responded on all sides to different site conditions. A site-sensitive building, one that escaped easy understanding from a single point of view, would mirror IBM's newfound capacity to react quickly to competitive shifts in the global marketplace.

Reading the complexities of a site is one of an architect's primary responsibilities, especially when the commission calls for a building to physically embrace the landscape. In Armonk, we made many attempts to find a solution that would fit the site. We settled on a challenging location where the terrain prompted dynamic rather than static form, where the building had to reach out and grasp the site like a mountain climber.

Two of the site's diagonally facing promontories offered platforms that could support the wings of our structure. By straddling the ravine between the promontories with a bridge-like structure, we reduced the amount of rock excavation. The bar-like volume joined the two anchoring wings at each end, which faced in opposite directions and together with the bar formed a Z-shaped configuration. Like a captain's bridge, the linking piece became the locus from which Mr. Gerstner and his key executives collaborated with teams working in the wings.

Dimensionally, the three pieces of the Z-shaped plan could be adjusted to create different types of workspace that could realign and transform IBM's working method and culture. We first focused on how to plan the interior in a diagram that met the company's new organizational needs. At IBM's request, we fitted the linking bar with a central tapering circulation spine, siting private executive offices on either side of the corridor. The spatial organization mirrored the organization of the company's executive structure. The outer wings of the building, shaped as truncated wedges thrusting out into nature, were organized as open-plan spaces that could easily be reconfigured for changing workplace combinations.

Once we proved to IBM, and ourselves, that our diagram and strategy could achieve IBM's organizational goals, we were free to address other issues, including the building's formal expression. We pursued many studies, chief among them the building's physical response to the site and the image this building represented to the world of a reinvented IBM.

Mr. Gerstner's leadership and his aspirations for the forward leap of the company suggested a building with an aggressively athletic posture that radiated energy. The morphology that had emerged from our organizational studies suggested a lightning bolt, and by fracturing and fissuring its form in successive explorations, we increased the visual energy. We used action verbs such as twisting, thrusting and leaping to prompt us to achieve active form.

We first focused on the two pivot points in the Z where the ends met the middle at an angle: these were critical joints with spatial, formal and programmatic potential. We positioned spaces of social gathering at these special geometric moments—the main entry lobby, the boardroom, a significant conference room, and below the entry level, the main stair to the dining spaces. We made each of these sculpturally unique and expressive both inside and out. Programmatically and visually, they became the building's anchors. From these anchors the building's wings thrust outward, engaging the site with a physical energy that responded to the challenging terrain.

Marrying a building to a natural site suggested the use of natural materials, but IBM is an enterprise about technology not nature. Bridging the divide between nature and technology required an ingratiating transition. To mediate the two worlds, we selected a rough, hand-laid fieldstone for the building's base. Having created a bond to the earth, we clad the building above in a material that expressed technology—bead blasted stainless steel—which contrasted dramatically with the stone base. We heightened the sculptural expression of the tapered forms by extending the roof surface at a pitched angle toward the woods. The roofs too are clad in the same stainless surface that covers the building's vertical surfaces. The canting, slicing, and twisting roofs join the vertical walls of the building to complete the sculptural dynamic of the building as an organic whole.

We can't really claim that our design was responsible for IBM's success under Mr. Gerstner's leadership. But perhaps we helped achieve two of architecture's important goals, creating a sense of enjoyment for employees, and a sense of community: the design helped change the corporate culture. It also projected an image that identified and clarified the company's aspirations.

This building is now over twenty years old. Looking back, I have very few design regrets: we have the satisfaction of knowing that we would now do little to change it. Long after the tenure of the executives who hired us, the buildings still speaks to the same issues—the dynamic nature of a progressive corporation, and the nature of nature.

Gannett/USA TODAY Headquarters

McLean, Virginia, U.S. – 2001

Site plan

Gannett/USA TODAY commissioned KPF in 1992 to design a high-rise for a newly acquired site in McLean, Virginia, within a suburban office park, Tysons Corner. The project didn't turn out the way anyone expected.

Tysons Corner is home to many corporations. Each corporate building follows a model, which has become, sadly, dominant within this type of development—a multistory static structure surrounded by a field of parking. The model is economical and efficient but devoid of human spirit. Our "comparative process" that we had come to employ as a method to uncover our aspirations and our clients' led us, step by step, away from this point of departure to the building we finally designed. Our clients' appreciation of the architecture over the last twenty years gratifies me deeply.

Alberti's words, "The city is like a large house, and the house in its turn a small city" spoken in the 15th century, was my inspiration for Gannett: a corporation is a small city, too. Creating a pleasant working environment for a group of people with a common purpose would enhance their ability to create the news and their enjoyment while collaborating.

Much has been said about creating community through architecture. To me, the physical act of "gathering together" is paramount. The more casual the interchange this type of building can generate, the greater the chances of forging bonds for teamwork. Anticipating the act of gathering through every step in the design was key to precipitating it.

Large newsrooms, in which journalists work together closely, played a dominant role in the brief. Gannett and USA TODAY were each to have its own space. A newsroom is a highly social place with continual face-to-face interchange. Large, roomy, unobstructed floors were needed to accommodate spontaneous group gatherings and more private one-on-one encounters. This requirement in itself ruled out the usual office-park model of a single tower sitting on a larger base, with a central vertical circulation core discouraging interaction. Vertical circulation needed to be placed outside the confines of the newsroom, but immediately adjacent to it.

Furthermore, Gannett and USA TODAY each had an identity of its own, yet a mingling and bonding of the two corporate cultures within common social spaces was both desirable and possible. Instead of creating two competitive towers in a face-off, we thought of bringing two structures together like hands clasping. Each company wanted to share social spaces such as lecture rooms, dining areas and a common entrance lobby, scaled for grand receptions, media events, and dinners of the type well known in Washington, D.C.

As we developed crude massing studies, our understanding of the desired functional relationships emerged, which changed the preliminary thoughts for the form of the nascent structure. But why do studies before fully understanding the programmatic relationships? Design is never linear: in our process, we always end up pursuing many dead ends before reaching a full understanding of the issues. In McLean, what now seems, in retrospect, to be inevitable certainly was not when we began. It was a process of search and discovery.

Context plan

What finally emerged was a common vertical, functional stacking diagram of two linked volumes. The lowest floor, devoted to shared functions (such as an auditorium, cafeteria, etc.) initiated the stack. Above this common entry level, we positioned two separate floors of newsroom space, each 90 feet deep. This depth guaranteed access to natural light and dimensional flexibility. And, by extending each newsroom toward the other, we hyphenated the newsrooms and achieved a communicative linkage. Surmounting these newsroom floors were several levels of office support space. Here, we reduced the office depth to 60 feet to augment the penetration of natural light within the offices.

The functional diagram resolved, we then turned to the site. The property was situated adjacent to the intersection of two main arteries, the Washington, D.C., Beltway and the Dulles Toll Road. The adjacency was ideal for vehicular access, but the traffic noise required buffering. The site was shaped like a bent bar. Each arm sloped down to their joinery at a regional drainage basin. This potential water feature divided the 30-acre site into two roughly equal portions, one on the southeast and one on the northwest. Each section was evaluated as a possible building site. Steeper, beautiful, and more wooded, the southeast portion at first seemed preferable, but it faced predominately north. The northwest site was more gently sloped and unwooded. Facing south, it guaranteed access to full solar exposure for communal spaces, inside and outside. The sun made the decision for us.

Then there was the always-difficult issue of parking. To save the site from being blanketed by 1,800 cars, our client generously agreed to build structured parking. We took strategic advantage of the requirement by placing an eight-story parking structure along the entire northwest boundary of our site. The long, linear building formed a strong edge to the site that separated us from a visually aggressive neighbor. It also created the possibility of a garden-like passage between the parking structure and the building itself.

The stage was set for adapting the diagram of the building to the site. We simply took our stacked volume, one part for Gannett, the other for USA TODAY, connected by a link, and bent it in a U-shape around an expansive exterior south-facing room. We inflected each bar of space slightly. At the inflection point we placed two glass-enclosed elevator towers opposite each other, allowing each half of the company to see its counterpart moving between floors. The towers generated main lines of circulation within the building, activating the building's perimeter facing the communal exterior room.

At every formal opportunity, we sought to create a sense of spontaneity, energy, and tension between the building's dominant volumes. The angled geometric complexity of prisms sliding and interlocking dynamically enlivened the highly rational planning strategy. The landscape architect Michael Vergason reinforced the angular interplay, extending the energy into the gardens with a cascade of linear fieldstone bars, inspired by the patterns created by logs floating down a river, terracing down to the lake.

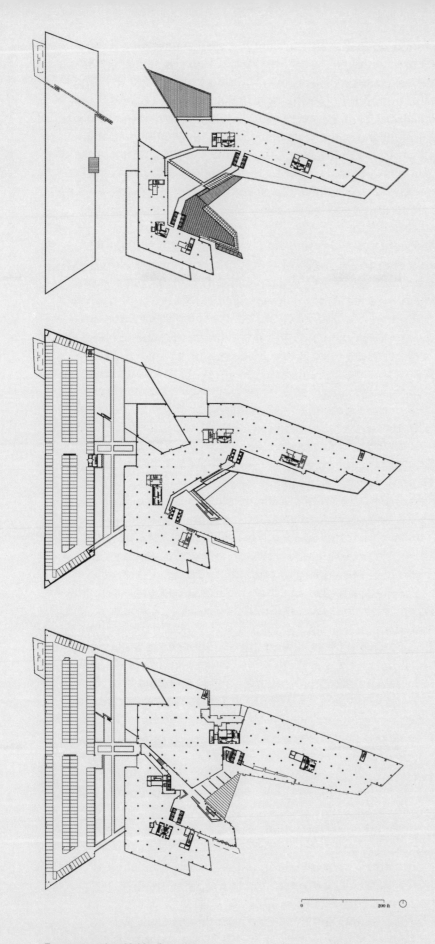

0 200 ft

Tower, second and lobby floor plans.
Opposite: north and south elevations

The visual energy of the complex is made almost ethereal by the lightly reflective glass of the façades, which created unexpected effects with light passing through. Mirrored glass is often overused, but we transformed the often-literal reflections with a dense space of vertical mullions 2'6" on center, a vertical glass fin attached to each mullion. Acting as a practical shading device, it refracts and reflects light, but beveled on their outward edges, the fins create spectral patterns of light penetrating into the interior spaces.

The architectural critic Joseph Giovannini said it best. "It is the vertical fins that initiate the effects of both indeterminacy and changeability on the façade. The fins generate a range of surface effects that transforms by the minute with the light. Collectively, the fins vaporize the façades, removing the harshness of reflective glass and producing ephemeral effects. The sun, like a slide projector, casts the rainbows inside, often striating walls and floors in fugitive patterns of color that shift and vanish as the sun moves or dims; environmental phenomena activate a façade that has been set up to shift in unanticipated ways. The fins that dimensionalize the surface with a sense of shadowy depth and unpredictable light, then, also animate the interiors."

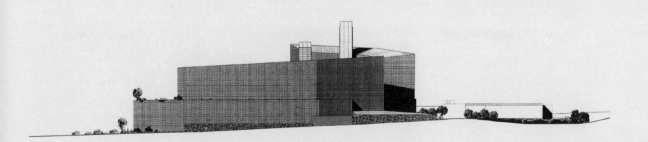

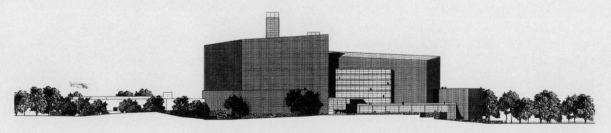

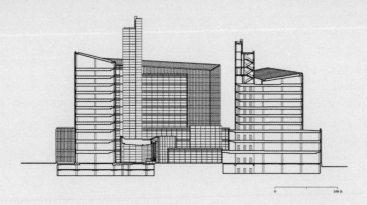

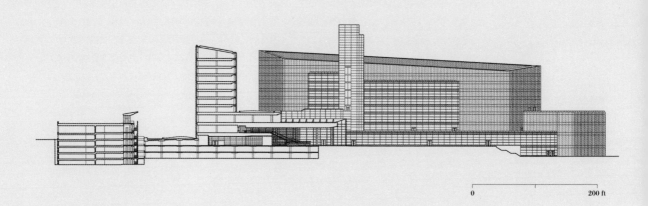

Cross section looking west and longitudinal section

Baruch College Vertical Campus

City University of New York,
New York, U.S. – 2001

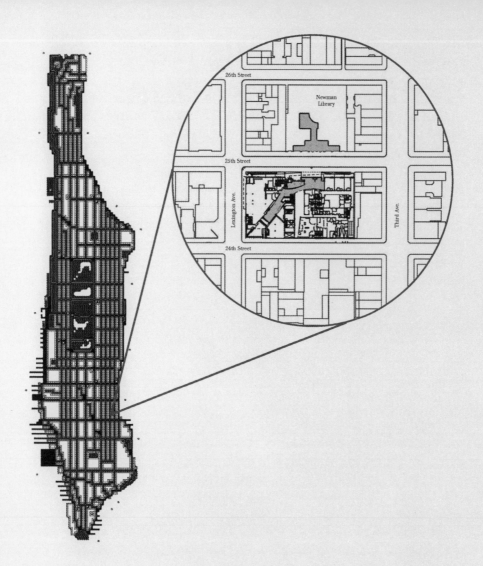

Within the circular site plan:

26th Street

Newman
Library

25th Street

Lexington Ave.

Third Ave.

24th Street

Context and site plan

The "Vertical Campus" is the most idiosyncratic of all the buildings I have designed in my long career. Built for Baruch College, one of the several colleges that form the City University of New York (CUNY), the hybrid structure contains, under a single roof, every conceivable type of academic space (other than residential). Occupying almost a full block on Lexington Avenue between 24th and 25th streets in Manhattan, the building has few precedents.

Dr. Matthew Goldstein, then president of Baruch and later the chancellor of CUNY, aspired to provide the student body, dominantly composed of the sons and daughters of immigrants, with a physical environment that encouraged vibrant intellectual interaction between students and faculty. Inside and out, we expressed his aspirations by mixing and interweaving diverse programmatic components. The result is a 14-story city-in-miniature (with three floors below grade) that houses 5,000 students in a "vertical campus."

New York City zoning allowed two options for building on this site. One was to fill the site entirely up to a height of 85 feet. Above this height a relatively slender tower, occupying only forty percent of the site area, could be built to the required height. The second option, the one we selected, again filled the site to 85 feet, but above any additional volume had to be set back 15 feet and lean back at a prescribed angle for its entire height. This option produces a lower, more compact mass. The deep floor plates that result make introducing natural light challenging, but they also enable a better mix of programmatic functions and more efficient vertical transportation for the large numbers of students changing classrooms.

A traditional college campus clusters the main academic buildings around a central quadrangle, which, in turn, becomes a type of town square enabling chance encounters and interchange. Our objective, within the dimensional limitations of a restricted urban site, was to create this type of social dynamic within a dense urban building that we tried to shape as a vertical campus. The vehicle that enabled this potential was a cascading, 13-story atrium bathed in natural light from top to bottom. This multistory room, linking together each of the academic functions, was punctuated every third floor by large gathering spaces. Each of these gave a social focus to the separate schools comprising the college. Level two is home to the Student Center; level five, the Weismann School of Arts and Sciences; and level eight, the Zicklin School of Business.

This three-story hierarchy is a product of a unique vertical transportation system, which is the backbone of the building. Solving this building's vertical transportation was our first priority, and we decided on a skip-stop primary elevator system that would bring occupants to every third floor. From these primary floors students and faculty ascend or descend a flight of stairs. (A supplementary vertical system is provided for those with a disability.) Each of the six main elevators holds 30 students and opens both front and back. The rear doors release before the front doors allow entry. The system, a form of mass transit, verticalizes New York City's subways system so familiar to all students and faculty, who usually arrive by train.

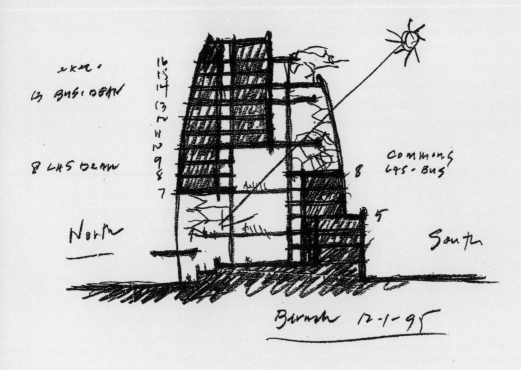

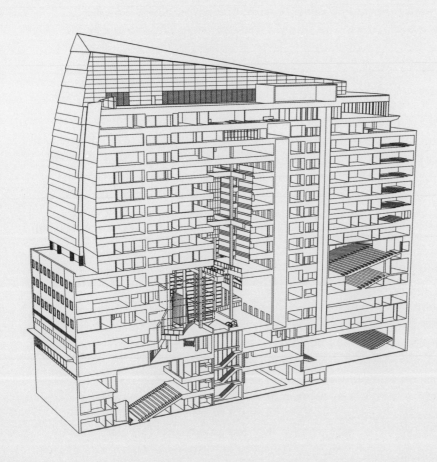

Bill's sketch and sectional perspective

The three-floor elevator sequence starts on level two, the building's "piano nobile." The result is an amazingly efficient movement of students, which becomes a social event in itself.

All 5,000 of Baruch's students ascend in this atrium, which starts just inside the doors on the north face of the building. The atrium rises in a stepped section, ultimately reaching for southern light through a south-facing windowed room on the eighth floor. The building's exposed orthogonal steel frame, clad in fireproof plaster, weaves through the atrium in a diagonal vertical migration from north to south following the path of the sun. The sunlight beams through the building from high in the south to low in the north. This atrium is the equivalent of the traditional campus quadrangle, but tipped vertically. All the school's separate departments come together here into a whole that is no less symbolic for being an active working space.

Athletics and performing arts facilities are separated from the academic upper body of the building in three stories below street level. Each of these functions necessitated the movement of large numbers of people. Since the facilities did not require natural light, their location immediately below the street facilitated access, which we achieved with a three-story fissure equipped with escalators and stairs for the large number of people entering and egressing the events. The athletic functions are located east of this divide, and the performing arts spaces, west.

The fissure itself is partitioned north-south by a translucent glass wall that creates an atrium dividing the athletic functions from the performing arts spaces, which each received different architectural treatments. In the undercroft for performing arts, we created a somewhat dark and mysterious experience that is theatrical in nature, in contrast to the light-filled atrium above. The descent into the space leading to the athletics floors is more utilitarian, with natural light penetrating from a south-facing window. Overall, the spatial demands of the basketball courts, swimming pool, black box theater, and recital hall required a large-span transfer structure that could carry the enormous superposed loads of the entire building. We solved the challenge with full-floor spanning trusses, unobtrusively imbedded in the structure above the basement so that they did not impede the use or flexibility of adjacent academic spaces.

The architectural critic and theorist, Kenneth Frampton, in his essay on the design of Baruch College, called the building a joinery of "hull and house." He was referring to Le Corbusier's 1923 marine metaphor of a building as a ship. Frampton represents Baruch as a type of "Leviathan berthed on Lexington Ave." While the curved upper body of this building does have the profile of a hull, its arched profile satisfying the zoning laws and setbacks, also echoes the famous 25th St. Armory, its close neighbor. Frampton's "house" reference alludes to the traditional brownstones that dominated the neighborhood up to the second half of the twentieth century.

Indeed we were explicitly making both these references. Masonry dominates the lower levels giving a more visually relatable

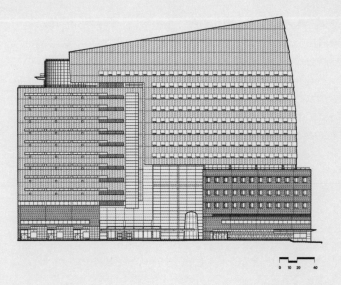

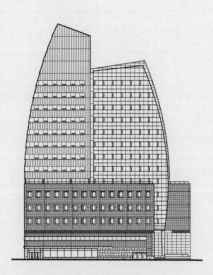

North, south, and west elevations

scale to the portions of the building closest to the human body and to the pedestrians on the street. The "hull" rises above this weighty base, dominated by a horizontal layering of fenestration tailored to the needs of the enclosed spaces. The western portion of the upper floors mostly houses faculty offices. Its shingled metal cladding is horizontally striated by fixed and operable fenestration. In the easterly portion of the upper body, composed largely of classrooms, a fenestration of high narrow windows brings a controlled light into spaces that require extensive use of electronic projection screens. Mediating these two lateral zones of the building are the large windows carved into the building's surface to introduce the natural light necessary to bathe the cascading surfaces of the central atrium. Perimeter staircases allow students to view the cityscape as they move up and down. From the outside, the building is an architectural collage that explains itself visually, expressing the different programmatic parts.

Kenneth Frampton concluded: "To the extent that the university is one of the last institutions capable of representing the body politic to itself, Baruch College may be seen as an exemplary labyrinth in which a whole world may be both enacted and represented. At the same time, it has been conceived as permeated by everyday life in such a way as to afford a passing glimpse of utopia as an end in itself."

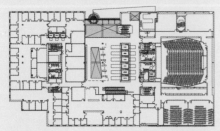

5th floor

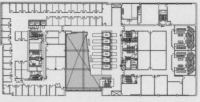

11th floor

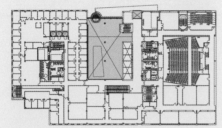

4th floor

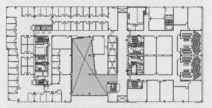

10th floor

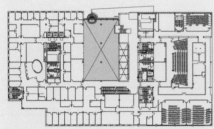

3rd floor

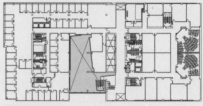

9th floor

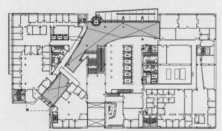

2nd floor

8th floor

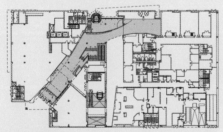

Ground floor

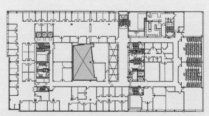

7th floor

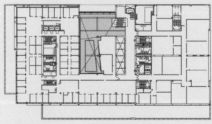

6th floor

VISTA MEDIA
Horizon Healthcare
Making Healthcare Work
GARDEN OF EDEN
FARMERS
JOHNNY FOX'S
GARDEN OF EDEN
GIFT BASKET
CATERING
FINE FOOD
GARDEN OF EDEN
GOURMET MARKET

Posteel Tower

Seoul, South Korea — 2002

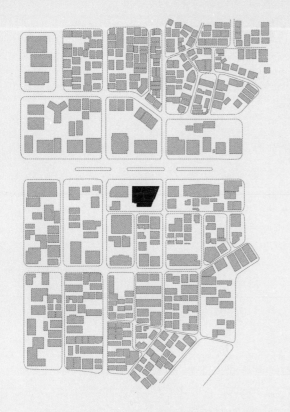

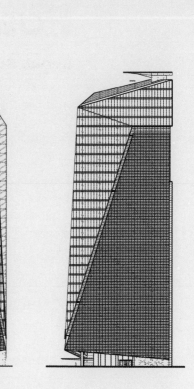

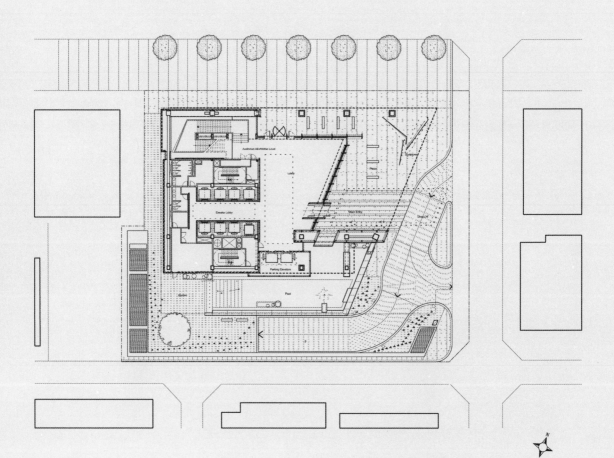

Context plan, east and west elevations, and lobby plan

The site in Seoul for Posteel, the domestic sales and marketing division of one of the world's largest steel companies, POSCO, was located on the capital's premier boulevard, Teheran-Ro, where many of Korea's major financial institutions are located, including the POSCO headquarters. Steel plate is one of POSCO's major products, and the Posteel Tower offered an ideal opportunity to feature its functional and esthetic appeal on a high-rise, while using the material to distinguish the tower from the neighboring high-rises.

Usually the design of a tall commercial building is driven by the external pressures of the context, but the Posteel commission had other drivers: an unusual site and several specific programmatic components, including a 300-seat auditorium and a helicopter landing pad on the roof. The buildable site area was so small and the size of the auditorium, so large, that the two factors became a strong impetus for conceiving the site strategy and the building's form. Moreover, given the site's prominent location along a street wall of high-rises, we wanted to punctuate the street architecturally with the equivalent of an exclamation mark.

The wide floor plates of many high-rises lead to bulky structures, but on Teheran-Ro, the relatively limited site, along with requirements to leave a large percentage of the site free and open, presented the unusual opportunity of designing a more lithe, more expressive structure. Towers of smaller scale and bulk are far easier to integrate into an urban context than are those with massive girth.

Zoning requirements made the site into a chessboard of requirements. Responding to one triggered moves that played out against other requirements, leading to an interdependent matrix of responses.

The first requirement was to set the building back along Teheran-Ro, which enabled us to align our building with others along the street. Respecting the setback at the street meant that we could design a tower without stepping back the shaft (until the final several floors). The alignment of towers along the street formed a wall that we wanted to respect and extend, but a zoning requirement that 50 percent of the site remain open actually worked against the continuity of the street wall. A building centered in a buffer of space suggested a large gap, one that would break the rhythm of the street wall between Posteel and its neighboring structure to the north.

Positioning the auditorium was key to unlocking the whole site and organizing the building parti. Placing the auditorium between the Posteel Tower and its northern neighbor resolved the contradictory goals of maintaining open space along the street and closing the gap between adjacent buildings. A wedge is an ideal shape for auditorium sight lines, and by siting the wedge-shaped auditorium at the northeast corner of the site, we deployed its geometry to both close down the gap and open the site.

The wedge's acute angle at the corner gave the site its starting point, allowing the entry wall into the building to angle into the site from the property line as it moved south. The angling wall of the auditorium allowed us to minimize the gap between the buildings while bringing the street wall along the full length of the property on Teheran-Ro. This diagonal east-facing wall liberated the necessary open space at the southern corner of the site. Furthermore, the acute angle at the northern corner on Teheran-Ro set up the geometric conditions we could develop into the urban exclamation mark we were seeking. Ultimately, we developed this acute corner as a type of lightning bolt hurtling to the earth. Overall the play of angles on the site chessboard cued responses in the tower's façade.

We positioned the auditorium opposite the structural core. The two components, auditorium and core, practically filled the entire usable site area, leaving between them a space that was not adequate for an entry lobby. To create sufficient space, we lifted the volume of the auditorium off the ground high to create a generous lobby below. We kept the area to the south of the core and the tower open, per the 50 percent open space requirement, and used the open space to create a vehicular drop off that included access to underground parking.

Our point of design departure into the body of the building was the entrance beneath the belly of the elevated auditorium. The inherent drama of this entrance could be heightened if the auditorium appeared to float overhead, independent of the walls of the tower plunging to the earth. We decided to separate the auditorium from the tower by including the auditorium within the building's enclosure, which gave the sense that the auditorium was shrouded.

The play of angles from the site into the building created virtual inflection points that fissured the tower into a faceted prism with two façades. One was horizontally striated, with delicately projecting louvers. These shaded and textured the walls. The second façade, flat and smooth, enclosed a corner volume that ascended from a point above the corner entry to the sky along a diagonal structural line. This formal gesture constituted a dramatic element of urban punctuation as it morphed into functional spaces for the cafeteria and dining floors at the upper levels.

Despite its drama, the bold slash up the façade defers to the play of angles along the street. A second diagonal gesture arrests vertical movement of the north-facing façade, keeping it from reaching the ground. Facing Teheran-Ro, this cross-gesture lifts the skirt of the building, and reveals the drama of the entry lobby while sheltering the entry. Within this space one experiences the soffit of the auditorium above and the escalator movement within the lobby, while seeing a dining area in a sunken garden below grade. Massive stonewalls enclose the garden, anchoring the space within the earth while heightening the sense of the tower's lightness above. Thirty stories up, the tower responds to the sky with a dramatically sculpted helicopter landing pad.

Throughout the building we celebrate the use of steel, demonstrating its strength and bearing capacity through gestures that only steel can perform with such elegance. We put into practice what POSCO sells. But the product placement was not an end in itself. The use of steel reified the architectural gesture of our exclamation point. As a dramatic urban marker on Teheran-Ro, it heightens the imageability and legibility of the city and facilitates wayfinding. Designing a point of urban reference, a theatrical landmark, has made a large and complex city more memorable and humane.

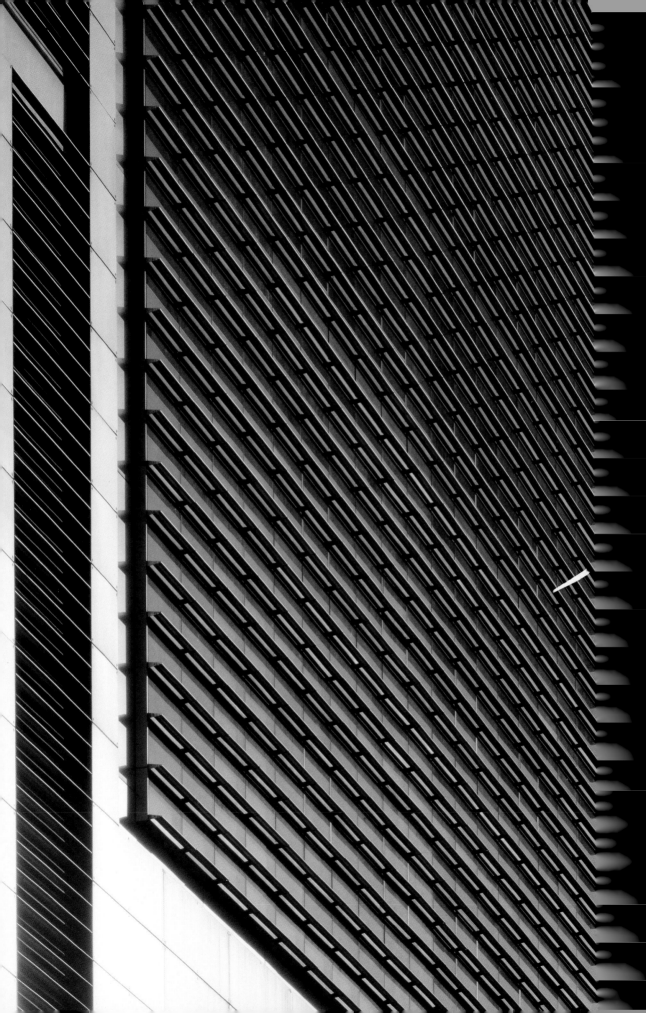

Shanghai World Financial Center

Shanghai, China — 2008

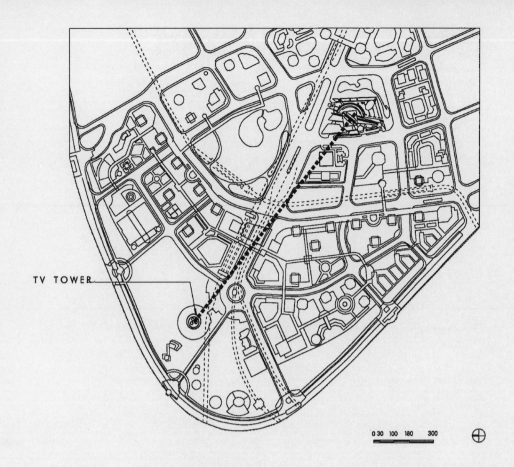

TV TOWER

0 30 100 180 300

Context plan

Our commission for the Shanghai World Financial Center in China originated in Japan, where we had worked with Minoru Mori and his company, Mori Building, on a large, mixed-use development in the center of Tokyo, Roppongi Hills. Mr. Mori asked us to collaborate again, this time on what was to be the world's tallest building in Shanghai's emerging central business district, Pudong.

The Chinese government had dedicated Pudong, which lies just east of the river that runs through the center of the city, the Huangpu, to encourage international commercial development. In 1995, when we started the project, the urban development plan included over 80 commercial towers, the lowest 40 stories. Pudong was rapidly becoming one of the biggest construction sites in the history of the world, and it already claimed what was then the world's tallest structure, the Oriental Pearl TV Tower.

Our site was one of three adjacent parcels that urban master planners had designated as sites for super-tall buildings. One, the pagoda-like Jin Mao Tower, by the American architectural firm SOM, had been designed during height of Post-Modernism.

Two sites remained vacant, and ours was reserved for the tallest of the three buildings. Since it was to be called the Shanghai World Financial Center, we decided to search for a form that would express China's rapidly rising position in the international economy. The building had to earn the name.

Jin Mao's patterned historicist texture, though well done and evocative, was so specific and self-referential that we decided to relate to it by contrast, in a conversation of opposites that would juxtapose the rough and the smooth. Our building could still be based in Chinese history, but through other references and forms.

We found roots in ancient China. Considered abstractly, a very tall building connects the earth and sky, an idea best expressed by a design that appears lighter as the tower rises. The ancient Chinese had symbols for both earth and sky, and in ceremonial graves, they placed artifacts representing the passage from earth to the heavens. The artifact recalling the earth was a square shaft of dark stone striated with carved horizontal lines. The corresponding artifact representing Heaven took the form of a circular disc of smooth, almost pure white stone, its center carved as a circular void, creating a flat doughnut shape. These two artifacts inspired our architectural search for a similar passage from earth to sky.

As at Jin Mao, our tower housed two main programs, a hotel built over an office structure. Each required floor plates of different dimensions and geometries. The office component needed greater depth, and the most efficient form is the square. However, a central core surrounded by a generous depth of flexible office space generated dimensions too deep and inefficient for the hotel above. Jin Mao dealt with this geometric misfit by carving out a great atrium in the hotel. We looked for a more efficient solution. Given the visual cacophony of Pudong, we felt our building, the tallest, should be the most serene, and that a form of purity and even nobility would quiet the surrounding visual noise. We tried to design this urban stabilizer by connecting the geometries of a square below and a circle above.

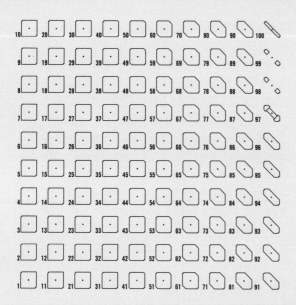

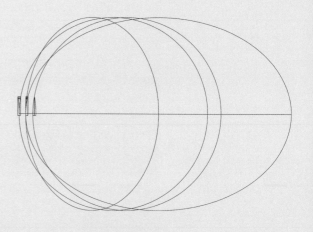

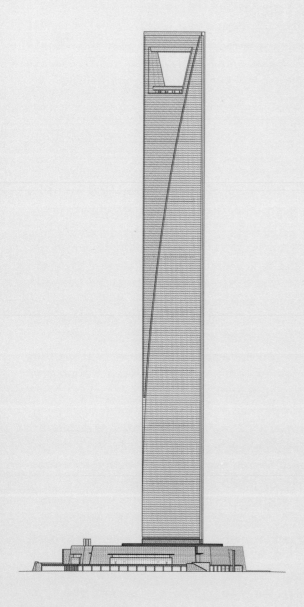

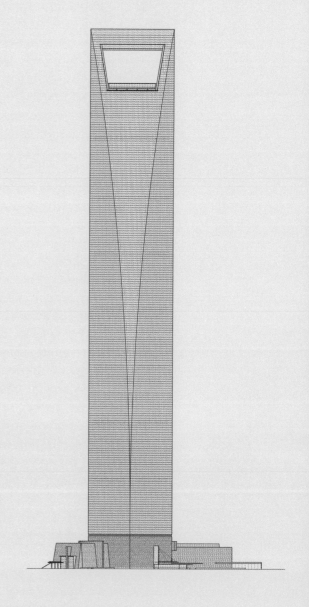

East and north elevations

Just before beginning the Shanghai World Financial Center, I was commissioned to design a simple door pull that was intended for commercial production, and my design concept for the handle influenced the Shanghai design (I find that working at small scale informs large-scale work, and vice versa). For the handle, taking a pure cylindrical form as a base, I allowed the grasping motion of the human hand to shape the pull as an intersection of two geometries, one form static and the other its reciprocal form, dynamic.

In Shanghai, different geometries intersected. I drew two arcs of sweeping dimension through the base form of a square prism, the shaft that represented a 500-meter-tall building. Starting about a third of the way up the shaft, the curving arcs rose from the opposite outside corners of the prism and splayed out as they moved upward until they connected to the other two opposite corners at the top of the prism. The arcs formed an arching plane within the shaft fore and aft, the square shape of the building in plan giving way to a curving oblique plane that rose with the height of the shaft. The gesture, symmetrical on the front and back façades, reduced the size of the floor plate in the upper reaches of the tower, reconciling the dimensional disparity of the square footages required for the offices below and the hotel above. Like the grasping motion of the hand on my door pull, the arcs intersected and carved the prism.

Physics entered the design equation. The overturning forces of the wind are actually more dominant in the design of very tall buildings than the compressive forces of their weight, and the wind suggested the possibility of a large void near the top of the structure to decrease overturning pressures particularly intense in Shanghai's typhoon season. The monumental sphere atop the nearby Oriental Pearl TV tower implied that the void in our tower echo the sphere as a circle, establishing a reciprocal urban connection in the sky.

For us, a circular void at the top of our building recalled the ancient stone discs representing heaven, and it also recalled the traditional moon gates in Chinese gardens. To the Chinese, however, it represented something else, as I learned when I presented the design to 14 Chinese professors of architecture who were responsible for its review and approval.

Each professor was given thirty minutes to respond to my ten-minute presentation. The first to speak was an elderly woman with a kindly demeanor. She spoke the only words of English during the day, other than mine. She began by saying, "Perhaps this building is acceptable, but it certainly isn't desirable."

I was floored. Everyone to whom I had shown the building had responded positively. Our client loved it. But as comments by the professors continued through the morning, the tone was ominously ambivalent. Still, no one was specific about the objection. At lunch break we recessed to an elaborate meal featuring live shellfish, each squirming on the serving plates. We were to sever the creatures with our chopsticks. The meal seemed symbolic, and made me think of my experience in the morning's jury, where I was the subject of the chopsticks.

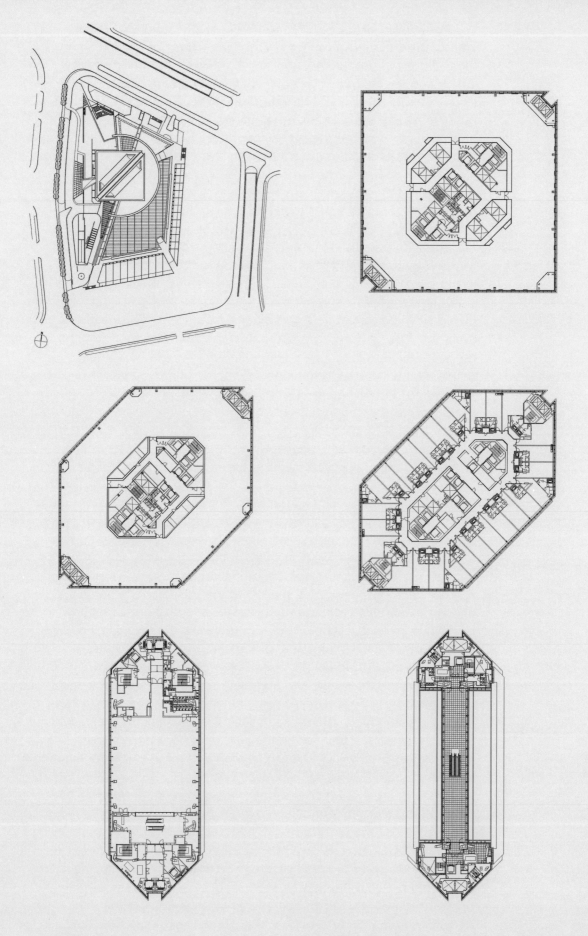

Top to bottom from upper left: roof plan, low-rise office plan, high rise office plan, hotel plan, observation plan (94th and 97th floors)

But even after the day's review, we never learned the real source of the problem. Only a month later in a newspaper review did we learn the reason: "Japanese developer comes into Shanghai with the flag held high." To us, the circular void referred to a Chinese artifact with a sublime meaning, but to our hosts, it represented the Japanese flag, and all the more so because the tower was Japanese owned.

Our well-intended disc in the sky threatened the approval process. To receive approval, we needed to defuse the international political implications caused by the circle. Later, at an emergency meeting in Tokyo with Mr. Mori and the mayor of Shanghai, I proposed a bridge within the circle, symbolizing the joining of two sides (and, unfortunately, denying the purity of its geometric form). The alternative was initially accepted, but eventually rejected, and I finally moved the bridge to the top of the tower where it became our main observation deck. Below it, we transformed the circle into a large trapezoidal opening.

We still had our opening, and though its form changed, it performed an equally effective role in releasing the pressure of the wind—and a much more effective role in releasing the pressure from politics. And, it would be easier to build.

Soon afterwards, approval for construction was granted, but just as the work of driving the long foundation piles into the unstable earth was almost completed, the Asian financial crisis struck. The project lay dormant for five years.

When the project was resumed, changes were made, chief among them Mr. Mori's decision to increase the height and width of the building. Building on the piles already driven, however, was impossible since as built, they could not take additional weight, and adding more was prohibitively difficult. Leslie Robertson, the famed structural designer of tall buildings, was brought in to re-evaluate the structure. Employing a composite design of super columns, outrigger trusses, and diagonal bracing, he was able to reduce the unit weight of the building enough to allow for the additional height and breadth. He also produced a design that was more efficient to build.

None of the structural changes affected the basic concept and shape of the building, which some observers have charitably likened to a Brancusi because of the clean simplicity of the evolving shape. The purity of the form even survived some after-the-fact pragmatic alterations. The most significant occurred on the lower levels where a large retail facility was added, which led to the design of three distinct entrances at the building's base, for office, hotel, and retail. A long powerful diagonal stonewall was introduced slicing through the base, creating a powerful organizing element for the entrances. Each entry type was given a unique character and identity that expressed its role. A fourth entry penetrating the stone base was added for tour buses bringing the many visitors to the observation deck at the building's top. This portal dramatically penetrates the stone base. The American designer Tony Chi was brought in to design the interior of the Park Hyatt Hotel occupying the upper portion of the building.

Other than the major entries, no penetration was required into the heavy stone base anchoring the tower. We dramatized the visual weight of the building's connection to the earth with a cladding of roughly textured gray granite. Its power was amplified by its simplicity. We glazed the full height of tower's shaft rising up from this anchoring base in a lightly reflective glass that was horizontally striated by semicircular mullions. Reflecting both natural and artificial light, the evenly spaced mullions dramatized the building's form day and night.

For several years the Jin Mao Tower and the Shanghai World Financial Tower stood together in a respectful relationship awaiting the presence of the third and final building. Originally planned to stand at a height between that of the two existing structures, the Shanghai Tower was finally built to a much greater height, the third in a trio of super-tall buildings whose critical mass collectively transformed the Shanghai skyline.

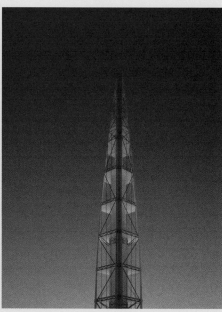

Samsung Seocho
Headquarters

Seoul, South Korea — 2008

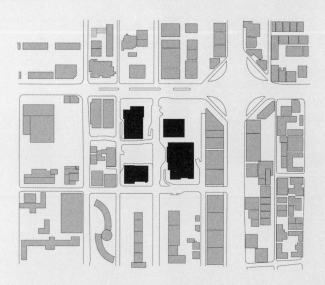

Top: Context plan
Bottom: Interlocking wooden blocks

One of my favorite architectural stories involves a conversation between Eero Saarinen and Phillip Johnson. The two had just participated in an event, with many other architects, where they were asked to create compositions out of colored tiles. Coming out of the room together Johnson said, "Those colors were so awful that I only used the black and white ones". Saarinen replied, "I only used the white ones."

This is somewhat related to our experience designing the Samsung Electronic Headquarters in Seoul, Korea. Over the years we had developed many compositional strategies for our buildings introducing non-orthogonal relationships. Early buildings rely heavily on the relationship between linear and curvilinear geometries. Buildings such as 333 Wacker Drive in Chicago and the AAL Insurance Headquarters in Wisconsin reveal a very specific attitude about the dialog between the straight and the curved line. It is a dialog similar to that expressed between the parts of an archer's bow; the curve of the bow and the straightness of the cord. Over the years fluidity became more prevalent in our work. Jackson Square in New York is a good example of this. Angularity too played an increasing role beginning with the Gannett and IBM buildings. It was also prevalent in my house on Shelter Island and Hudson Yards in New York. These non-orthogonal geometries were fundamental to our ability to express a formal architectural response.

Here, in the design of the Samsung Electronic Headquarters, these options were taken away. It was made very clear to us, at the beginning of the design process, non-orthogonal geometries were not to be used. Trying to explain our case was not really possible. The edict had been passed down from the chairman of Samsung. We, as architects, had no access to him. Our architectural tool box was reduced to that of just the white tiles. This building was to be a composition of rectangular forms.

Our site, in downtown Seoul, was zoned for the inclusion of three high rise structures. They could be composed in a grouping similar to that of Rockefeller Center in New York were it not for the fact that a major street bisected the site. This made impossible the creation of a space of gathering which drew all three buildings together. Adding to the complexity of our challenge was the presence of a holdout structure which occupied a critical position at the entry to the complex.

Of our three buildings, two were designed to provide space for the Samsung Group. These were offices for the suppliers/manufacturers that service Samsung. The third was to be devoted to the new Samsung corporate headquarters. It was to contain a major showroom for all the products Samsung produces—a Samsung Museum.

Despite the presence of the city road bifurcating the site we were determined to create a relationship between all the buildings which enabled them to speak to each other. Intent on inspiring gesture we evolved a massing strategy of interlocking parts. It was a method of volumetric composition which could be compared to that of traditional Korean woodworking. The interlocking of rectangular wooden blocks was the essence of this ancient esthetic. While

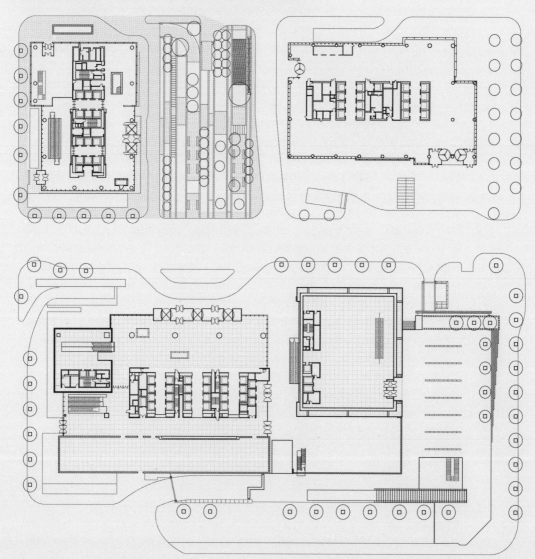

Section and ground-floor plan

working at a far different scale we achieved the same objective. This strategy enabled us to separate the larger mass of each tower into three or four individual parts. Each part became a building within a building. The geometry of these parts formed interlocking vertical L-shaped volumes made independent by large reveals separating them. These reveals enable the individual pieces to appear to float in space. They were made necessary by the unique Korean system of positioning air handling rooms directly on the perimeter of a tall building. (Centralized systems, requiring large mechanical floors, were minimized by the presence of these decentralized, floor by floor, systems.) Each room, on an individual floor, is contained behind a horizontal air intake grill three meters in width. Stacked together, the air-handling rooms form a vertical slot enclosed by a horizontally striated metal grill recessed within it. In turn the slot enables the separation of the two wall types. It is a mediating element without which the wall types could not be given their independence. Within the main corporate building one of the reveals was expanded in dimension. This created a spatial void between the pieces. Here a stacked series of atriums were inserted, giving each floor a social center, encouraging group communication.

The articulation of each of the interlocking volumes inspired a textural response which enabled their independence almost like the alternating striations of wood grain give to separate interlocking blocks of wood. Our orthogonal volumes were deeply scored either horizontally or vertically. Each had a dominate grain direction. The scoring was given a depth of scale by a unique Korean requirement — the presence of numerous operable windows on each floor of a high rise structure.

The development of a wall type uniquely capable of expressing the dynamic of a building's compositional intent is always our goal. Much of our work, as designers of tall buildings, is focused on that objective. In our work this is made more necessary because of the gestural language we employ. The surface of a building needs to reinforce its volumetric intent. Here the interlocking of orthogonal volumes was the compositional strategy. To strengthen the physical character of the parts their interplay was reinforced by a weaving of horizontal and vertical surfaces.

Frequently, in our work, we have created a weaving of our building's surfaces. However, the weave is usually made possible by the materials which hold the glass. This time we created the weave predominately with the glass itself. Bands of it, 1.5 meters in width, were either vertically or horizontally composed. The flatness and independence of the glass bands glass was created by recessing a deep slot between them. This slot was utilized for the placement of either horizontal or vertical operating windows. These were demanded by the Korean building code. (To our knowledge it is the only building code which required them in commercial construction.) Ironically, had it not been for this requirement our wall type would not have been "discovered." But it was and it integrates powerfully with the volumetric composition. Without it, the dynamic of the interlocking volumes would be diminished.

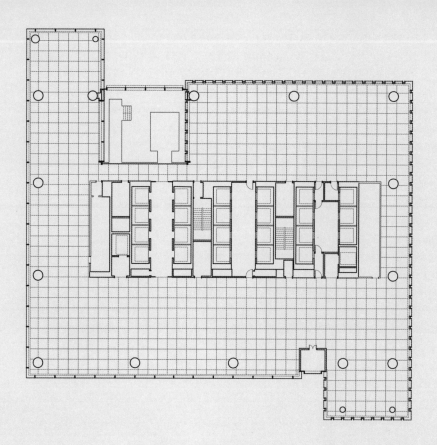

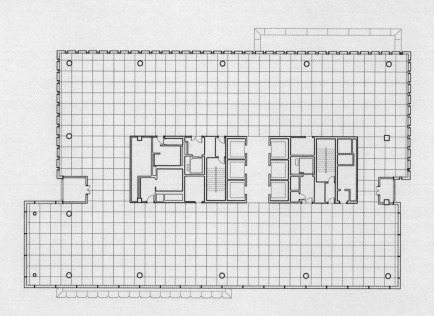

Typical office plans

Within the corporate headquarters building, on the easterly block, the concept of weaving was introduced into the public circulation on the lower levels of the building itself. A through-block passage penetrates east-west separating the Samsung Museum from the tower's main vertical transportation lobby. Enclosing the museum are clear glass walls minimizing the evidence of their support. They are transformed into glass veils intended to make more dramatic the objects held within. Facing north to a landscaped plaza, designed by Peter Walker, the museum acts as a backdrop to a space intended to embrace a variety of changing programmed activity.

Further heightening the sense of its connection Korean cultural associations the landscape also makes reference, on the plaza joining the north and south towers on the west block, to the concept of traditional Korean woodworking which lies behind that of our building's composition. Tiered interlocking levels of wooden blocks sponsor intimate seating within a canopy of overhanging trees. The inference that Samsung, a world leader in advanced technology, also values the crafted products of the human hand speaks eloquently of their corporate aspirations.

Clockwise from upper left: north, west, south, and east elevations

280

281

One Jackson Square

New York, New York, U.S. – 2010

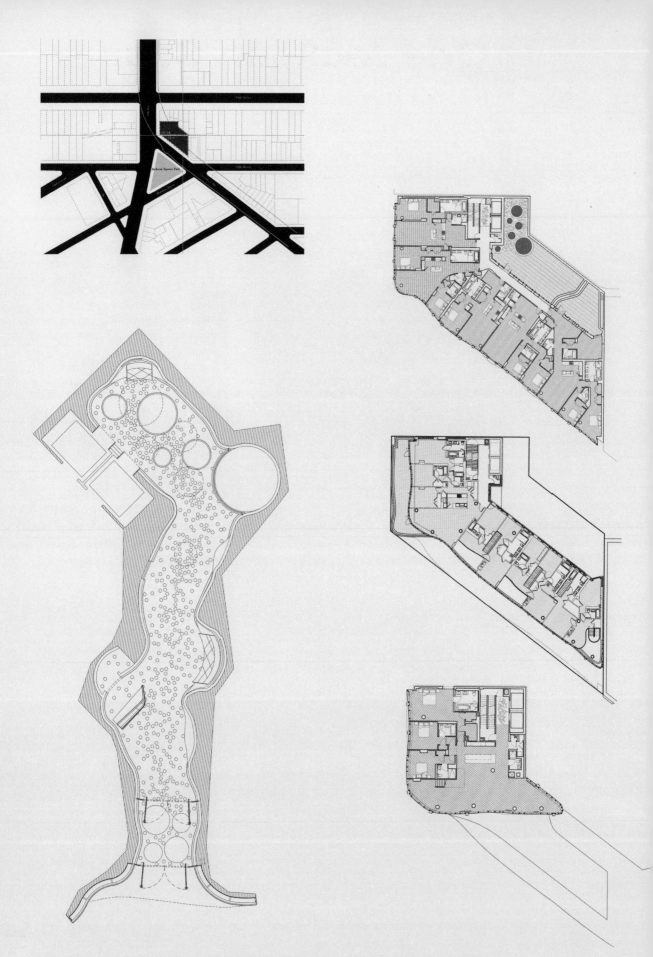

Top: context plan. Above, clockwise: lobby plan, typical apartment, duplex, and penthouse floor plans

Home to many artists, Greenwich Village in the 19th century became one of the world's Bohemian capitals, known for counter-cultural lifestyles set in its charming neighborhoods of tree-lined streets and brick buildings. In the 20th century, with artists like Andy Warhol calling it home, the tradition continued, and the offbeat neighborhood attracted residents who valued the scale, history, and aura of an old, storied village surrounded by a metropolis of skyscrapers.

For almost eighty years an oddly shaped site along one side of the triangular Jackson Square at the northern edge of the Village stood awkwardly vacant. After the Eighth Avenue subway was built through the middle of it, the infrastructure underground made construction difficult and prohibitively expensive. By the turn of the millennium, however, Greenwich Village started attracting wealthy New Yorkers, and land values increased. Development was feasible.

But receiving approval for building on the site, especially for a contemporary design, would be contentious. In the 1960s, Greenwich Village was landmarked, and the site stood within the historic district at its perimeter. Villagers were justifiably proud of their neighborhood, and they were vocal and organized. They liked brick and didn't like glass. And they didn't really like change.

Complicating the site's awkward footprint at the edge of a triangular "square" was its split zoning. The property straddled two zoning districts, each allowing different building heights—eleven stories along Eighth Avenue and seven along Greenwich Avenue. The law was effectively acting as a designer, but it was producing awkward massing.

My architecture has always responded to surrounding buildings through gestures that initiate a conversation. Here, however, zoning limited gesture, as did the market's demand to maximize building area. Subtracting mass as a way of inflecting the design was not a design option.

Besides the awkward and difficult site and the developer's expectations to maximize the site, materials proved another challenge. We were building in a neighborhood virtually carpeted in brick, but today's residential market prefers floor-to-ceiling glass for maximum views. Our commission was not unique: over the last 30 years, glass has been the rule in both residential and commercial buildings. How on Jackson Square could we design a distinctive building and yet contribute positively to the masonry fabric of the neighborhood?

Gradually we understood that the awkwardness of a zoning envelope built in glass was an opportunity with architectural potential. The incongruity of form and material might complement and even extend the idiosyncratic environment of Greenwich Village.

Shortly before receiving this commission, Trent Tesch, a young colleague, and I competed on the design of a hockey arena in Newark, New Jersey. As a former hockey player (for the University of Minnesota), I understood the fluidity of skating, and tried to express the weaving movement of the game into the building's form.

With the notion of fluidity on our mind, we started to think of the zoning envelope like a rock in a stream eroded by water over time.

The strange shape of the building required by zoning encouraged us to amplify the unusual character of the site by expressing fluidity within the mass. We could multiply the effect by eroding each floor so that the façade was striated with horizontal streams of glass.

Fluidity on a façade is more easily drawn than built. Weaving glass waves into the façade required that each floor be visually independent of the others. Therefore the outer profile of each slab had to vary floor to floor, with the bottom of each window wall standing at the edge of a slab. The top of the glass would either step back from the edge or protrude out on a horizontal ledge extended from the slab.

The protrusion allowed us to contour each floor independently, but the different contours meant the vertical mullion spacing couldn't align across the vertical layers, and that the glass panes would vary in width (which worked out to be 18", 24", and 36"). Building the waves of glass added another layer of complexity to the façade, another layer of eccentricity that agreed with the idiosyncratic character of the Village.

We studied the degree of reflectivity and the color of the glass for solar loading. But we took the idea beyond energy considerations into its esthetic impact on the square. We calibrated the glass wall, made up of flat individual panes of glass set at slightly different angles, to generate kaleidoscopic "play back" reflections dappling the surrounding masonry façades.

The Landmarks Commission understood our goals and strongly supported our glass building over strenuous, orchestrated community opposition.

We took the façade's fluid geometry into the building's entry. Here Trent took the lead digitally, conceiving this passage to the building's elevators at the back of the site as a gorge eroded and sculpted by the movement of water. CNC machines milled layers of laminated bamboo into complex curvilinear geometries that allowed us to create benches and other amenities within the flows of its surface. Starting directly behind the exterior glass, the wood draws people into the building in an ingratiating gesture of welcome. The warm architectural embrace of the sculpted wood entrance suggested craft, but the craft was achieved, from concept to execution, though digital technology. The entry established a precedent for future exploration.

The challenging zoning envelope and the fluidity of the interwoven façade had consequences inside in the uniqueness of each apartment. The façade wasn't simply extruded up from the building's footprint, and the variable massing and fluidities between and within floors produced a variety of apartments. Each apartment differed from the others because of some idiosyncrasy deriving from the building's shape. Low in the building, the apartments enjoyed close views of the park. Duplex apartments with terraces facing Greenwich Avenue topped this zone. The tower apartments were transformed into half- and full-floor units looking down on the surrounding city. All seemed informed by the unique genius loci of Greenwich Village.

Science Teaching and Student Services

University of Minnesota, Minneapolis, MN, U.S. – 2010

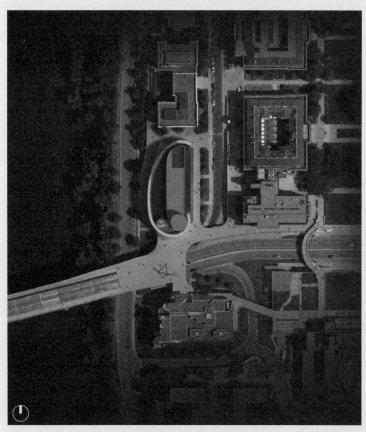

Site plan

After graduating from the University of Minnesota in 1961, I left the state, but over the years always harbored the ambition to build for my alma mater. When I told I.M. Pei in the late 1960s that I intended eventually to return to Minnesota to start a practice, he advised me to stay in New York and build in the Twin Cities from New York. At the time, it seemed only a remote possibility. I.M.'s advice proved prescient.

The campus of the University of Minnesota, on the east bank of the Mississippi River, was laid out in a master plan designed by Minnesota native Cass Gilbert. He originally intended to extend the axis of the campus mall from the library down to the River. That ambition, however, was never realized because the student union was built at the far end, denying Gilbert's powerful gesture of connection. In the late 1950s the University started building on the west side of the river, adjacent to downtown Minneapolis. Over the next fifty years, new construction there eventually exceeded the size of the campus on the original east bank. Developing both sides to a point of near equality raised talk of linking them functionally by programming Washington Avenue Bridge, which connects the two campuses (it's a long walk over the Mississippi, especially in a Minnesota winter). But nothing came to fruition. Short of that, campus planners realized that the two sites on the east bank on either side of the bridge could be designed as a gateway celebrating entry to the east campus.

Frank Gehry designed the Frederick R. Weisman Art Museum on the first site. Highly sculptural, with complex geometries clad in stainless steel that glints in the sun, it became, at birth, an instant landmark whose façade alone immediately signaled that it was a place for art.

Several years after the Weisman's completion, the opposite site became available. Campus planners decided to replace the temporary structures built there after World War II with a structure housing sciences and student services. We were invited to interview for the project.

It was the opportunity I had been waiting for. To my eyes it was the best site on the campus and maybe the best site I had ever had the opportunity to work on. We were awarded the project on the basis of our conceptual approach: If the Weisman was a building for art, I articulated how the STSS should be a building for science.

A duality suggested by the program led us to realize we could find and cultivate opposing conditions that would generate a design built on a dialogue of opposites.

The first set of oppositions was programmatic. Spaces for the teaching of science had very different needs than those for student services. At the time, the university was adopting theories of Active Learning Classrooms. In practice that meant developing classrooms fitted with multiple circular tables for groups of nine students, with roving instructors leading and monitoring discussions between them. Students at separate tables interacted together, with multiple video monitors for information spotting rooms carefully controlled for natural lighting. Movable walls allowed the combination of

Center: North and south elevation; bottom: west elevation

classrooms. The program called for four rooms of seven tables each. Traditional tiered lecture halls were included to create a mix of classroom experiences and pedagogies in the building. We assembled all the classrooms into a discrete volumetric stack of five floors that, clad in brick and facing the east campus, had a closed architectural expression that facilitated the control of natural light.

The second pair of oppositions was site specific. The east classroom side faced the masonry-clad campus, while the west opened to the Mississippi River and the Minneapolis skyline. The western orientation encouraged openness, but the exposure itself, with its heavy solar loads, challenged our desire to open views of the river. There was no such view opportunity on the east side, and therefore little temptation to open a form whose program encouraged containment.

The third pair of oppositions was symbolic. Together, the Weisman Museum and our structure would form the gateway to the east campus. The two buildings, one for art and the other for science, needed to talk. They needed to be copacetic, but different. As a pair, they could be Fred and Ginger.

Angular, sculptural, dynamic, and self-assertive, the Weisman wanted a more serene architectural companion, and we took our cue from the fluidity of the river, fashioning a mathematically inspired façade that captured its slow, linear movement while opening to the dramatic view and protecting the building from the sun. A fluid vertical space behind this façade opened to each of the floors, occupied by student services.

We matched the folded stainless steel planes of the Weisman by using polished stainless for our river-facing façade, striating the façade with a vertical columnar progression of glass. The spacing ranged from dense to open, depending on solar exposure. The façade oriented mostly west but curved at its ends, facing south directly toward the Weisman and north to its neighbor Appleby Hall. The mathematical relationship of the façade's vertically glazed openings suggested science, as the Weismann's sculptural façade suggested art. The openness of the vertically striated stainless steel façade enclosing student services contrasted with the east-facing façade of the science classes.

In all our academic buildings we simultaneously minimize the use of elevators and emphasize stairways in order to cultivate the social exchange of students moving through a building. Stairs and landings bind the primary programmatic components of the building into an active social whole that helps form a student body.

The use of stairs as our main conduit for vertical movement was made possible because of the building's relationship to grade and its main level of entry two levels above off the Washington Avenue Bridge. In this five-story structure, the entrance is at the middle level where we could introduce a large circular void that connects all of the building's levels. This void focused on a stunning piece of mathematical sculpture created by the St. Paul-based artist Alexander Tylevitch. A generous circular stairway rotates around the sculpture, with landings connecting to the informal study spaces.

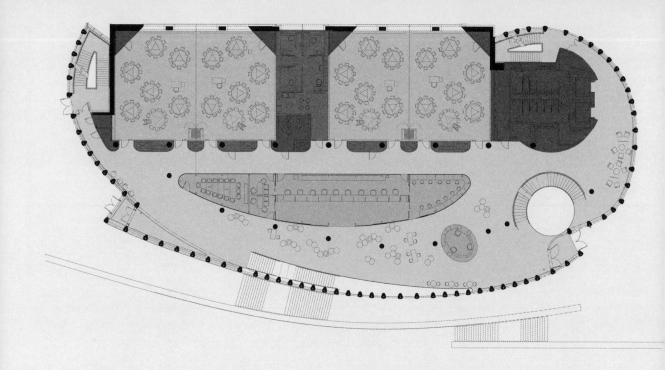

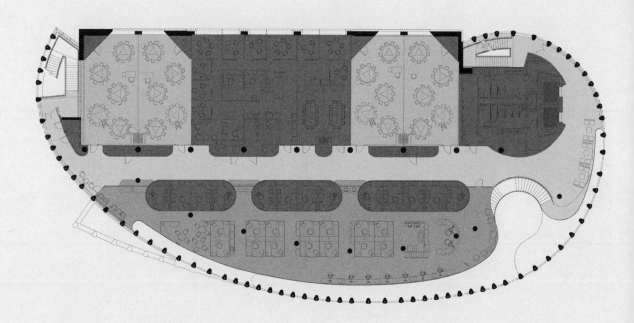

Top: Third-floor plan; bottom: Fifth-floor plan

Always full of students, these spaces face directly toward the Weisman Museum and the Washington Avenue Bridge's entry to the campus. The atrium and the campus outside enjoy a reciprocal visual relationship, the campus urbanism moving inside to become the building's interior urbanism.

After its completion, this building became a model for the architectural support of science teaching methods, setting a standard that has drawn visiting academics from around the world. The academic performance of its students validated the spatial organization and the formal expression that supported it. Equally important to us was the empirical evidence. Students found it was a wonderful place to hang out.

Receiving this commission from my school was worth the wait.

Transverse section

International Commerce Centre

Hong Kong, China — 2011

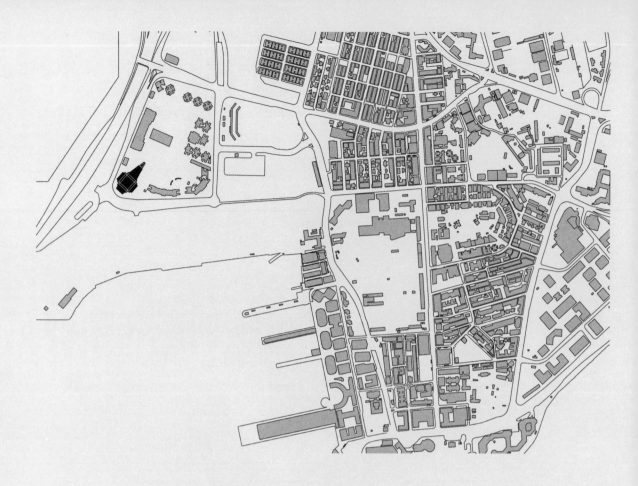

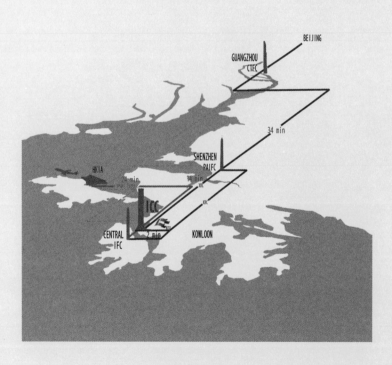

Context plan and China high speed rail link

The view from Kowloon Peninsula across the harbor to Hong Kong Central has always struck me as vegetal. The tall buildings have grown vigorously, like stalks, layered up against the green mountainous peak as though climbing to seek the sunlight. The Hong Kong building code, which requires a specific number of sunlight hours every day in each of the living areas of a residential building, mandated the extreme slenderness of the residential towers, creating the overall appearance of a field of wildly competitive asparagus. The urbanism is surprisingly organic. No city has anything quite like it.

The proposed site of the International Commerce Centre was located at the tip of the Kowloon Peninsula as it extends into, and frames, Victoria Harbour, facing the urban riot of high-rise stalks opposite. Hong Kong's largest developer, Sun Hung Kai, had invited us to compete for a building intended to be Hong Kong's tallest structure, and while the location afforded extraordinary sustainability in the form of access to transportation—24 minutes from Hong Kong's International Airport, two minutes from Central across the harbor, 14 minutes from Shenzhen, 34 minutes from Guangzhou—the very idea of its great height drew direct inspiration from the view it faced, as though feeding off Hong Kong's urban energy. Our site also faced the super-tall Two International Finance Centre directly across Victoria Harbour. Its great height (415 meters) and simplicity distinguishes the tower from the field of sprouting residential structures climbing up behind to the Peak. It was the simplicity of Two International Finance Centre that led me to consider creating a building of equal simplicity, though of somewhat greater height (484 meters), so that together the pair could act as a symbolic gateway to Victoria Harbour.

As a New Yorker, struggling to get to our airports and to others around the world, I was always impressed by the efficiency of Hong Kong's transportation system when I arrived there: it feels like being whisked into a future century. Despite the density of a population packed into a small amount of land, the city is remarkably easy to navigate. Perhaps this functional efficiency led us to achieve a similar directness in our architectural assignment. We decided to maximize the structural and constructional efficiency of the tower's form and let the most efficient solution generate the basis of our competition proposal.

Les Robertson, the great structural engineer of tall buildings who had worked with us on the Shanghai World Financial Center and with I.M. Pei on the Bank of Hong Kong, advised us during the competition phase about how we might achieve our goals. His analysis of four possible geometric types—square, rectangular, cylindrical, and triangular prisms—was detailed, conclusive, and directive.

Given that wind forces are the dominant driver of structural response in a very tall building, especially in a typhoon-prone city, we assumed that the cylindrical prism would prevail since it presents the least amount of surface enclosing a given floor area. Les, however, explained that "vortex shedding" occurs as the wind passes around a cylindrical form and creates exceptionally high negative forces difficult to resist without supplementary structure. Of all our forms,

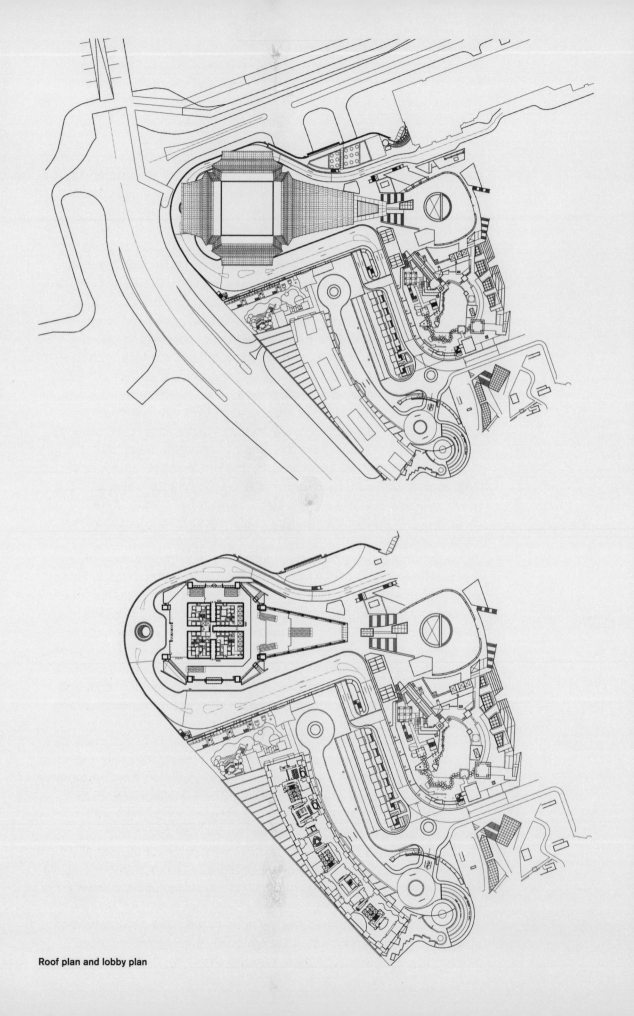

Roof plan and lobby plan

the square prism proved the most efficient, and the efficiency could even be augmented with "reentrant" corners that would break up the wind forces and reduce their impact. Les encouraged us to "confuse" the wind. The jagged edges of the reentrant corners were key to achieving the wind's confusion, therefore weakening its power to overturn the structure.

Years ago Les pioneered the concept of "super columns" in the design of very tall buildings, especially in a super-tall structure that is square in plan. In Kowloon, he suggested we position two massive columns on each of the building's sides, each column aligned directly with the outer edge of the building's core. The alignment enabled full-floor transfer trusses to connect at the mechanical floors to the external super columns so that the core and the columns were integrated into a single, highly efficient structural unit. The positioning of the eight super columns freed the four corners of the building for the reentrant geometry, doubling the usual number of corners to eight. The super columns, which freed the building's façade from the structure it enclosed, allowed us to design the façade as an entirely separate layer. Here the botanical reference of Hong Kong Central came into play as I pursued the idea of organic growth.

In the vegetable world a fruit is often protected by a rind or skin that, when peeled away, reveals the fruit inside. To me, the independence of the skin from the fruit was analogous to our aspiration for the building's glass cladding. If each façade was considered a layer applied to the structure, it could, in fact, be peeled away to reveal the structure. The reentrant corners could make each façade appear visually independent.

Detached from each other by the corners, the four surfaces could handle light differently both internally and externally, depending on the building's orientation. Experimenting with ways of minimizing nighttime reflections inside by tilting the angle of the vertical plane of glass, we found that pushing it outward at the bottom reduced reflectance. Furthermore, outside, tilting the lower portion of the glass outward increased the reflectance of the sky. Tilting the glass floor after floor produced the effect of a shingled wall in a textured façade. By extending the shingled glass planes past their intersection with the reentrant corners, the planes achieved a sense of visual independence from the building's volume. Together they created the building's enclosure as four independent sheaths of glass.

The logic of shingling façades in glass led us to the most dramatic formal gesture of the tower, meeting the ground. Each of the four vertical shingled glass planes could be flared out to hover above the ground and create independent canopies over the entry of each of the building's sides. We designed these entries to lead into separate elevator banks. The side facing the harbor and Hong Kong Central, was reserved for the entry to the Ritz-Carlton Hotel, located on the upper floors of the tower. There it was positioned above the 360-degree observation deck on the 100th floor.

The most prominent canopy faced Kowloon Station, which is the heart of the train transportation network connecting to the whole region. Here we created a huge sweeping gesture that extended the

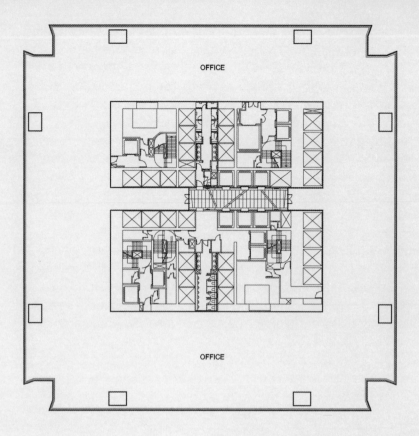

OFFICE

OFFICE

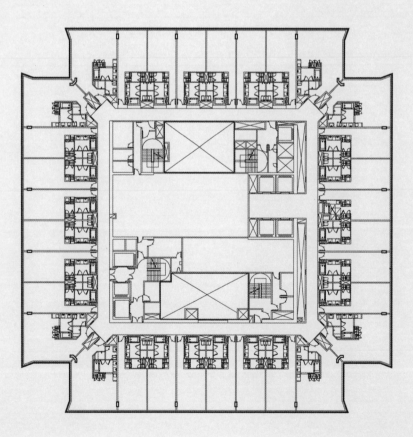

0M   5M   10M

Typical office and hotel plan

plunging vertical façade well beyond the footprint of the building in a long, sustained, sloping, nearly horizontal gesture of welcome.

The meaning of the word "Kowloon" in Chinese is "Nine Dragons." In Chinese Feng Shui the dragon is a "protector blessed with power, strength, wisdom, and auspicious energies." Its symbolic resonance in Chinese culture encouraged us to evoke the idea of a dragon's tail, represented by the sweep of a glass structure enclosing the primary entry to the tower from the access to public transportation below. Overt symbolism is not beyond our aesthetic boundary. Despite our commitment to, and interest in, formal architectural abstraction, our Shanghai World Financial Center was based on symbolic form, as was the "Bird's Nest" at the 2008 Olympics in Beijing by Herzog and de Meuron. Feng Shui is a prevalent motivation in China and most particularity in Hong Kong, a fact I had previously learned the hard way when a design my client once admired—"a work of art," he called it—earned the disapproval of a Feng Shui master because it looked like a "beetle." (We lost the commission.) In Kowloon, we went for the dragon.

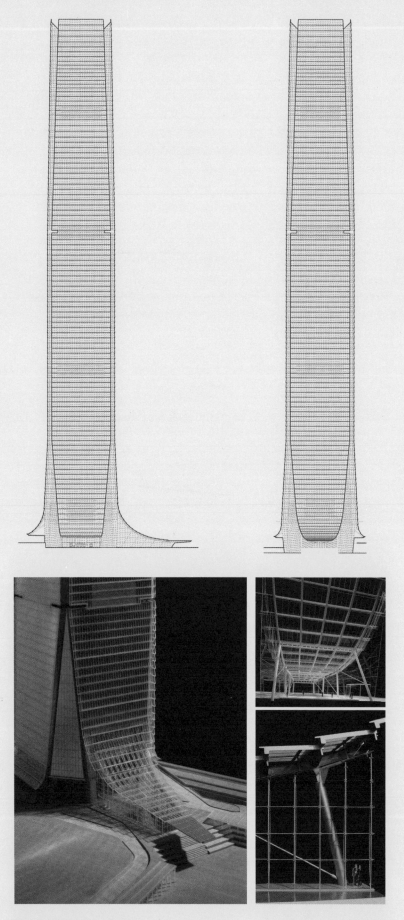

Top: east and north elevation
Bottom: model of dragon's tail

U.S. Courthouse Buffalo

Buffalo, New York, U.S. — 2011

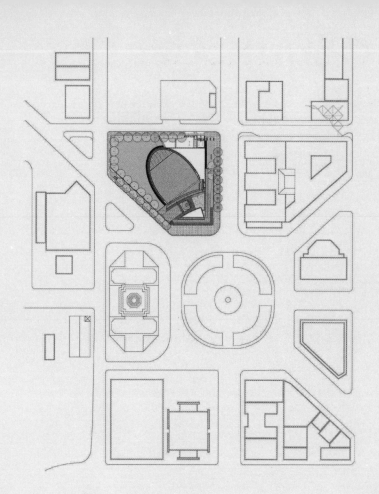

Context plan

After our design of the Portland Federal Courthouse in 1992, the regulations affecting the design of courthouses within the Federal Judicial system became increasingly stringent. In Portland, there were no setbacks needed from the property lines, but by 2001, the courthouse in Buffalo required 50 feet. This stipulation alone limited the available sites within the city to just four, from which we selected the most prominent and honored, a parcel adjacent to Niagara Square, the governmental heart of the city. The site also happened to be dimensionally generous. It offered many possibilities for architectural gestures that would integrate the structure into its architectural context and strengthen the urban fabric at this most critical point, the heart of its radial geometry.

Laid out in 1804, the plan of Buffalo was inspired by Pierre Charles L'Enfant's plan for Washington, D.C. The monument to President McKinley at the center of Niagara Square is the point of origin for the city's radial streets. President McKinley was assassinated in Buffalo at the Pan-American Exposition in 1901.

Facing the Square, City Hall—an imposing Art Deco structure designed by Dietel, Wade & Jones—is the dominant building, and a charismatic point of reference. Gesturing to this 1932 sandstone structure and to McKinley's monument at the circular center of the Square was an obvious design opportunity that would generate urban consequences that the urban spurs would transmit into the city.

The new setback requirements were really just part of the greater security regulations that had become more exacting since our work in Portland. A high percentage of the building's exterior wall now had to be designed to meet challenging blast requirements, a goal that was all the more difficult because the budgetary allowance for Federal Courthouses had been lowered. To accommodate the conflicting demands of a fortified building on a smaller budget, we conceived a compact design that reduced the area of the structure's perimeter relative to the amount of space enclosed. In what was a first for us, mathematics played a fundamental role in the design.

In my essay on the Portland Federal Courthouse, I described how the separation between the vertical circulation systems dominated the design. While the Buffalo courthouse is smaller than in Portland, the relationship of these primary elements, the circulation and the courtrooms, remained the same. In Portland, we discovered that two courtrooms per floor were ideal, and since our Buffalo site could not accommodate more than two per floor, that organizational format informed the basis of Buffalo's organization.

Examining alternatives of this format, through our comparative method, led us to apply the twin-courtroom strategy in a very different way. We evaluated each alternative simultaneously from both the perspective of its economic efficiency and its architectural and contextual potential. Gradually, less efficient forms evolved into more efficient schemes until an elliptical form emerged for the main body of the building. Instead of formally articulating such functional parts as the courtrooms and the

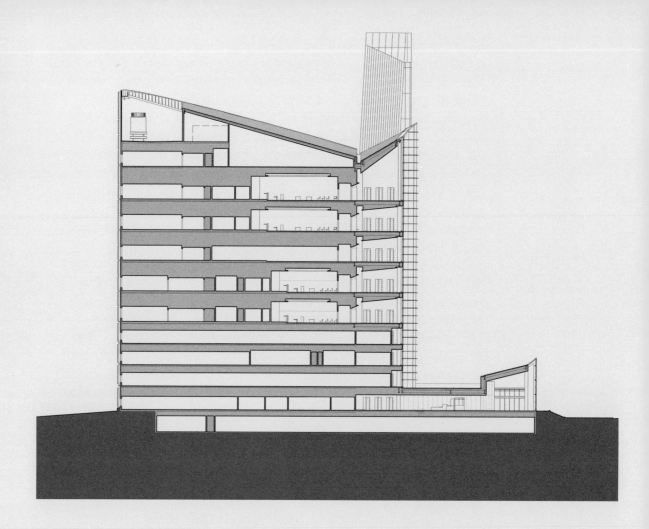

Section

judge's chambers, we brought them together into a single form, creating a unified shape that satisfied the structural blast issues, the reduction in the amount of exterior wall, and the reduction of solar load.

Resisting the forces generated by a localized explosion on the exterior of the building was our challenge. Our structural engineers recommended a ribbed precast external cladding that, if left exposed, would be inexpensive and structurally sound. The minimum surface area of the elliptical shape also increased the blast resistance benefit, and more importantly, its convex geometry afforded both a deflective capacity and an additional resistance to any blast.

Regardless of the shape, would the ribbed precast external cladding have sufficient dignity to represent the Federal judicial process? Our client didn't think so. We looked for a way to veil the frankness of the surface.

Employing the ribbed precast cladding as our exterior cladding and reducing the wall's perimeter area proved so economical that we had money left over to add a glass veil over the perimeter and still be within our budget. A fritted glass would further diminish the solar load. We had already reduced the impact of the sun by limiting the fenestration primarily to the judge's chambers, where we placed the windows to guarantee good views. (As in Portland, we brought natural light into the courtrooms by high windows over the jury boxes.)

The veil of glass proved a win-win solution. Connected to the wall with stainless steel clips and designed for sufficient separation for window washing and maintenance, the individual fritted glass panels animate and lighten the building's raw surfaces. Because we beveled the edges of the glass (as we had done in our Gannett building), the panels refract light and produce subtle but still dazzling spectral effects. Never had we designed a wall of such economy and elegance. I think of it as an invention in itself.

If we addressed the building's interface with the environment through the outer wall, inside we took great care to address the building's interface with the public.

As in Portland, generous, glazed public galleries on all the upper floors of the façade facing Niagara Square creates a psychological buffer zone releasing people into the view after coming from, or before heading, into the courtrooms, which we designed as highly efficient rooms that enabled an expeditious processing of justice within an ambiance of dignity and warmth.

As an active zone with people coming and going, the curvilinear façade of stacked galleries reads clearly to citizens on the street below, explaining visually how the building works. The gently curved, all-glass exterior surface of this gallery, expressed as a shield independent from the body of the building, embraces Niagara Square and responds to the circle within it. At its narrow end, the galleries thrust beyond the body of the building creating a dramatic place for viewing the surrounding city. At the other

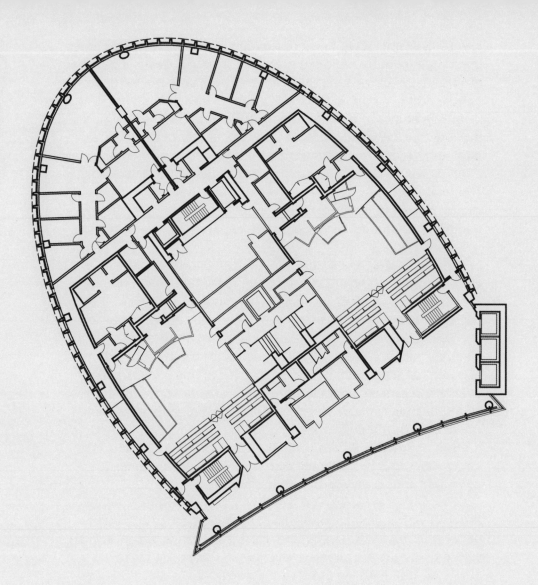

Typical court room floor plan

end of the tapering gallery, an elevator tower in a concrete shaft joins the façade of galleries as an architectural gesture with a civic presence, like a campanile. The tower anchors the urban composition, stakes out the building's presence in the skyline, and supports at its top a lantern seen in the night sky.

A third civic gesture is the trapezoidal entry pavilion, a semi-independent low-rise structure made entirely of glass and scaled to welcome rather than intimidate the public. One side fronts the main square as it holds the line of the street. All 4,536 words of the United States Constitution are written in a white fritted script on its surface. Facing the square, the text can be read by passers-by.

Inside, an inner curving glass side faces the sculpted architectural shapes of a courtyard. The pavilion holds several glass "paintings" done by the artist Robert Mangold, artworks whose colorful elegance adds a joyful note to the aura of gravitas that usually characterizes a courthouse.

The building's three semi-independent civic gestures—the wall of galleries, the elevator tower, the entry pavilion—speaks an architectural sign language that communicates a message that tempers the solemnity of the courtrooms and mitigates the psychological intimidation of a building in which people are judged.

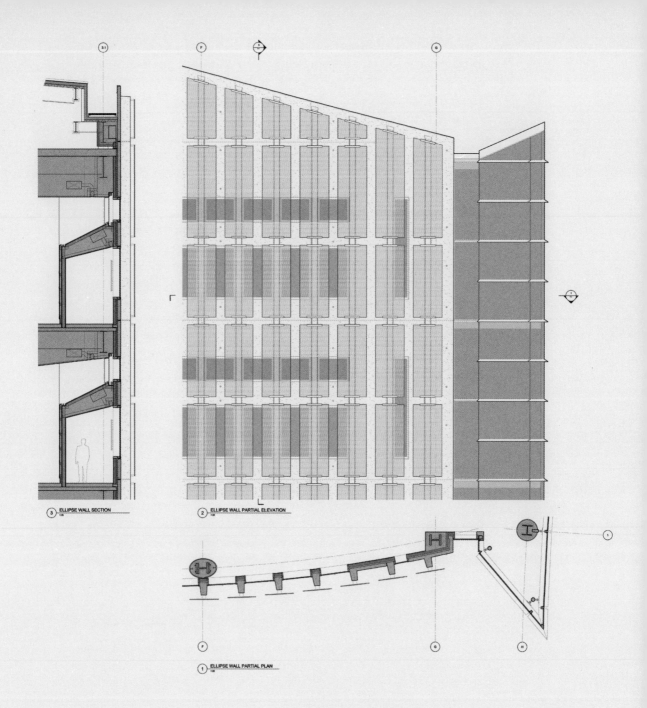

③ ELLIPSE WALL SECTION
1:25

② ELLIPSE WALL PARTIAL ELEVATION
1:25

① ELLIPSE WALL PARTIAL PLAN
1:25

Ellipse wall section, ellipse wall partial elevation and plan

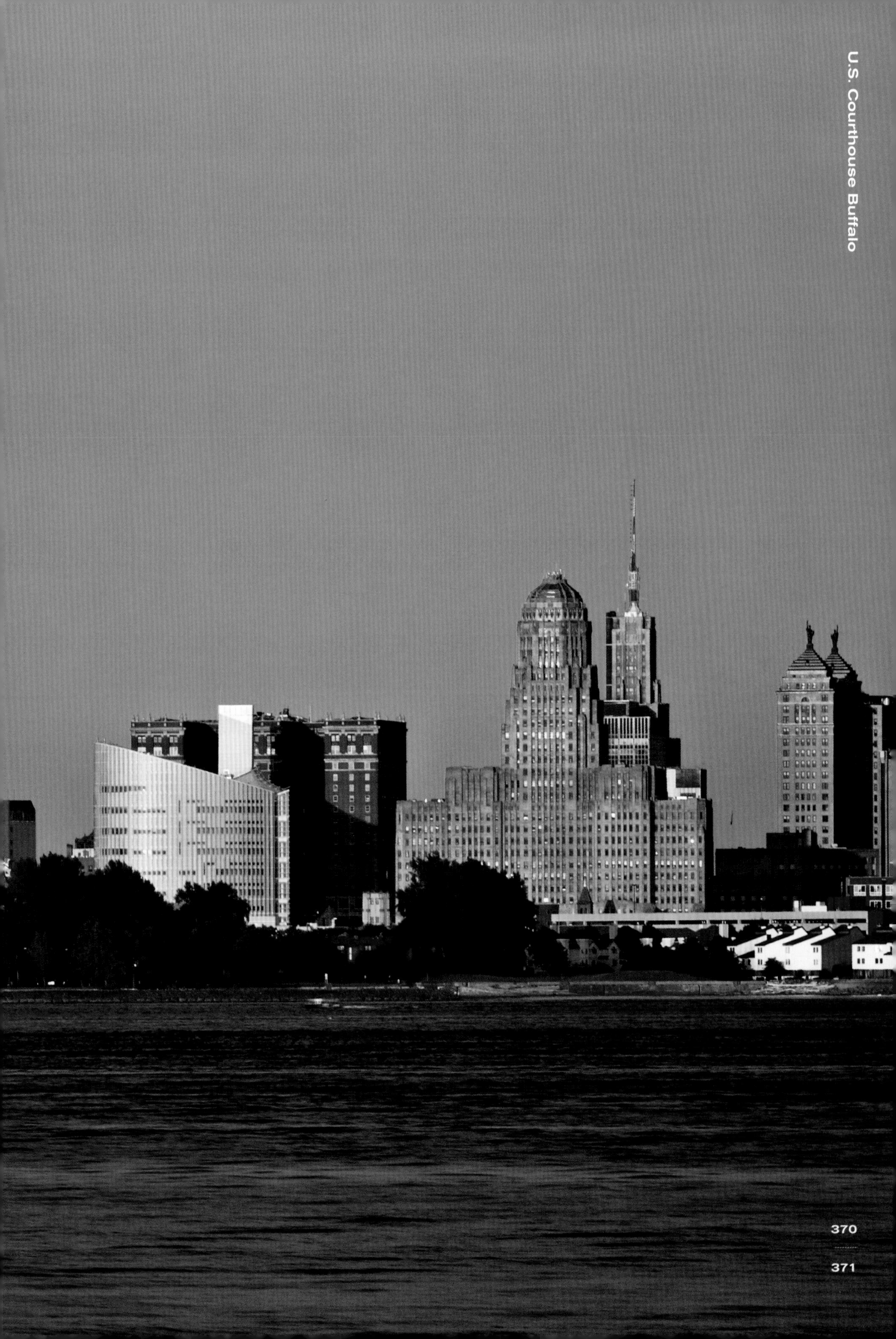

McCord Hall

Arizona State University, Business School
Tempe, Arizona, U.S. — 2013

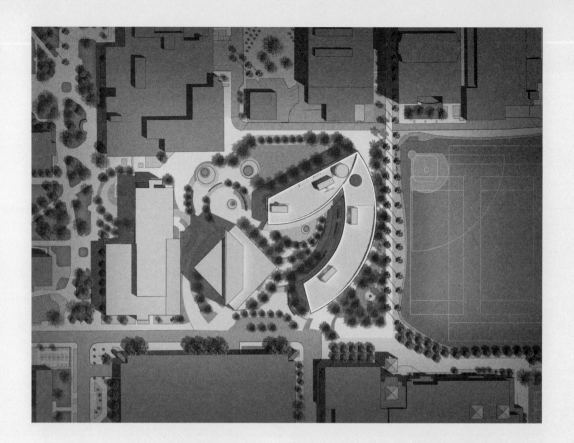

Site plan

For decades the academic institutions and business schools we designed in the United States were located in the country's higher latitudes, but in 2009, we were asked to double the size of the W.P. Carey School of Business at Arizona State University in Tempe, Arizona, by adding a classroom and administrative building, McCord Hall. The campus's relatively low solar latitude in the dry Southwest gave us the welcome opportunity to create outdoor public spaces that would drive the design. The challenge was to minimize solar loading to keep the spaces comfortable.

Choosing brick and concrete for the building was our first and easiest design decision. The materials were not only cost effective within the limited budget, but they also suited the character and feel of the landscape and the existing W.P. Carey School, which was built in brick and concrete (like much of ASU). A reddish brown colored, brick cladding concrete structure seemed perfect for a campus built in a semi-arid context. To control solar exposure, we would have to minimize the dimension of windows set in the brick fascia, and we would protect larger expanses of glass with densely louvered screens of steel. Never before had I chosen a building's materials before creating its form. The materials deeply influenced the design.

The existing W.P. Carey building was a strong cubic volume, which we used as an anchor for the alternatives that we developed by our comparative process. Its square plan, rotated onto a north-south axis, afforded south and west entry points into what would be an exterior room, the focus of the complex, walled by two new structures on either side. Concerned about creating a room that would be comfortable in the Arizona sun and one that moved the air, we shaped the outdoor room before designing the buildings that enclosed it, trying to produce a breezy Venturi effect. We created a triangular space with a concave concrete arm on each side that curved at the leading end into an open prow that generated a vortex which accelerated the flow of air and the flow of students and faculty coming off the main campus axis, Palm Walk.

Roofed with a curving brick mass punctured with a cylindrical oculus open to the sky, this dynamic portal is a grand entrance that invites people into the complex. At night, a spectacle of lights programmed in the oculus animates and dramatizes the moment of entry into the embrace of the courtyard's arms.

We developed the building's geometry and programming around the outdoor space, the heart of the building. Strategically, because classrooms placed on the lowest levels of an academic building relieve the pressure on elevators, we put most of the classrooms on the first two floors of the east-facing arm, and consequently needed only two elevators in the four-story structure. Its concave curvature proved ideal for the alignment of four U-shaped, 80-person classrooms on the lower two floors, which we front with multiple breakout rooms for group study. Students can access all these rooms directly from the outside, at grade, or from an exterior corridor on the second floor, access points at two levels that keep the courtyard active. On the outside of this wing, the four-story volume facing athletic fields forms a powerful backdrop to the largest open space

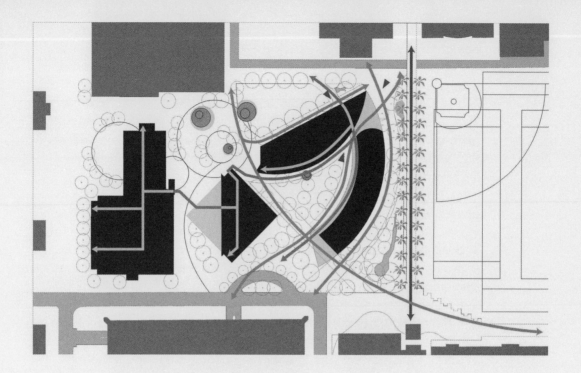

Circulation plan

on campus. Its mass and façade gives edge and definition to the otherwise loosely shaped grounds.

The other (western) arm, which contains the building's main entry and much of the complex's administrative space, has a courtyard-facing façade that is almost straight and acts as a foil to the fluidity of the curving geometry of the arm opposite. Exterior stairs enclosed with vertically grilled iron slats animate the façade.

The materials we chose, the brick and concrete, would play a big role in determining the school's architectural character, so we paid a great deal of attention to the texture of our brick surfaces, and the fenestration within it. We wanted to cultivate an architectural personality that was both contextual and unique, and of course we needed to respond to Arizona's severe solar conditions in order to achieve a high degree of sustainability. Our strategy was to leverage nature. In this case that meant taking advantage of the angle and intensity of the Arizona sun to create a play of shadows that patterns and textures the surfaces in light and shade. We discovered that vertically scored striations on the curving surfaces brought out the rounded shape of the building more than horizontal striations.

The wall elevations evolved through numerous compositional studies that included how the windows transmitted light inside. We learned that narrow slots of light had a strong animating effect within, and because most of the administrative spaces were relatively large spaces of open office landscaping rather than small individual offices, an array of narrow apertures, adjusted for lateral spacing and vertical height, cumulatively achieved a powerful collective effect. Outside, we celebrated the placement of the windows by corrugating the fascia with ribbed sections of stack-bonded brick that integrated the vertically striated fenestration. A metal blade projected from one side of each vertical window strip created shadows that rippled across the textured brick.

We introduced large surfaces of glass in only one zone, a two-story, curving area for casual seating located the westerly bar facing the exterior room. Solar control was critical to its comfort. The eastern bar opposite naturally blocked early morning sun. We designed a steel grillage constructed three feet in front of the glass to protect the interior from noontime sun. Finely spaced horizontal bars shade the glass from the high sun, and they project dramatic streaks of light that fracture the interiors in striated patterns.

The two new arms and existing cubic volume of the Carey school shaped the outdoor room, but we still had to design the room itself to accommodate both large gatherings and the individual student with a laptop. People always feel more comfortable along the edges of large spaces, so within the protective edges of the curved arms, we introduced curved linear seating on the plaza, sized at an architectural scale. We configured the seating to generate intimate zones for gathering, a strategy that generated a sense of rooms within a room. The curved geometry heightened the vortex-like fluidity of the space, augmenting its sense of dynamic energy. The outdoor corridor on the second floor overlooks the plaza like a balcony in a theater.

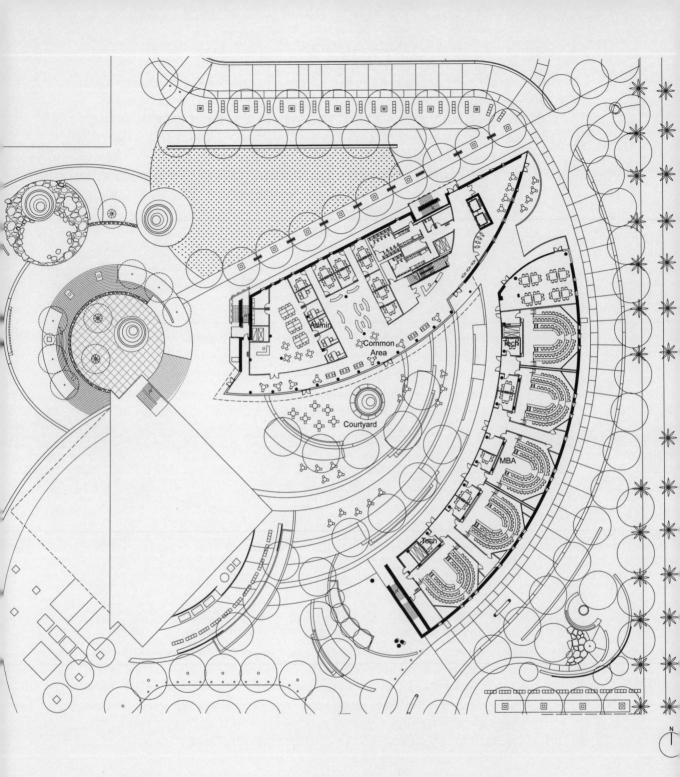

Admin

Common
Area

Courtyard

Tech

MBA

Tech

N

Ground-floor plan
Opposite: longitudinal section

ASU is a very large campus, but by forming a courtyard with the addition of two wings to the W.P. Carey School of Business, we created an outdoor gathering space that gives the school a sense of identity, and the campus a relatively cool, shaded and breezy refuge from the intense climate. Besides creating a comfortable outdoor space, our design offered the school a community room that socializes academic experience, emphasizing the human dimension of academia and learning together.

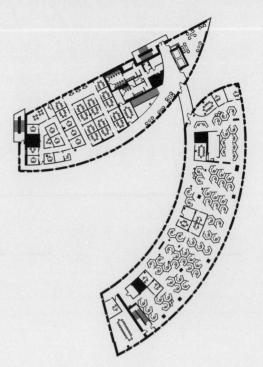

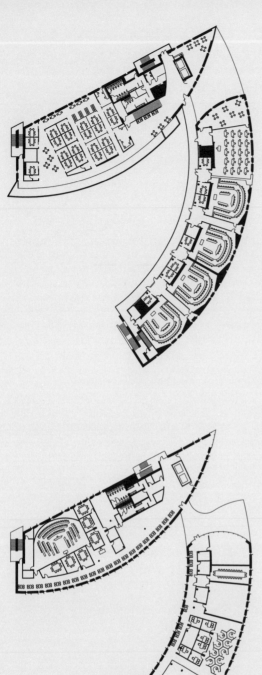

Second, Third, and Fourth levels

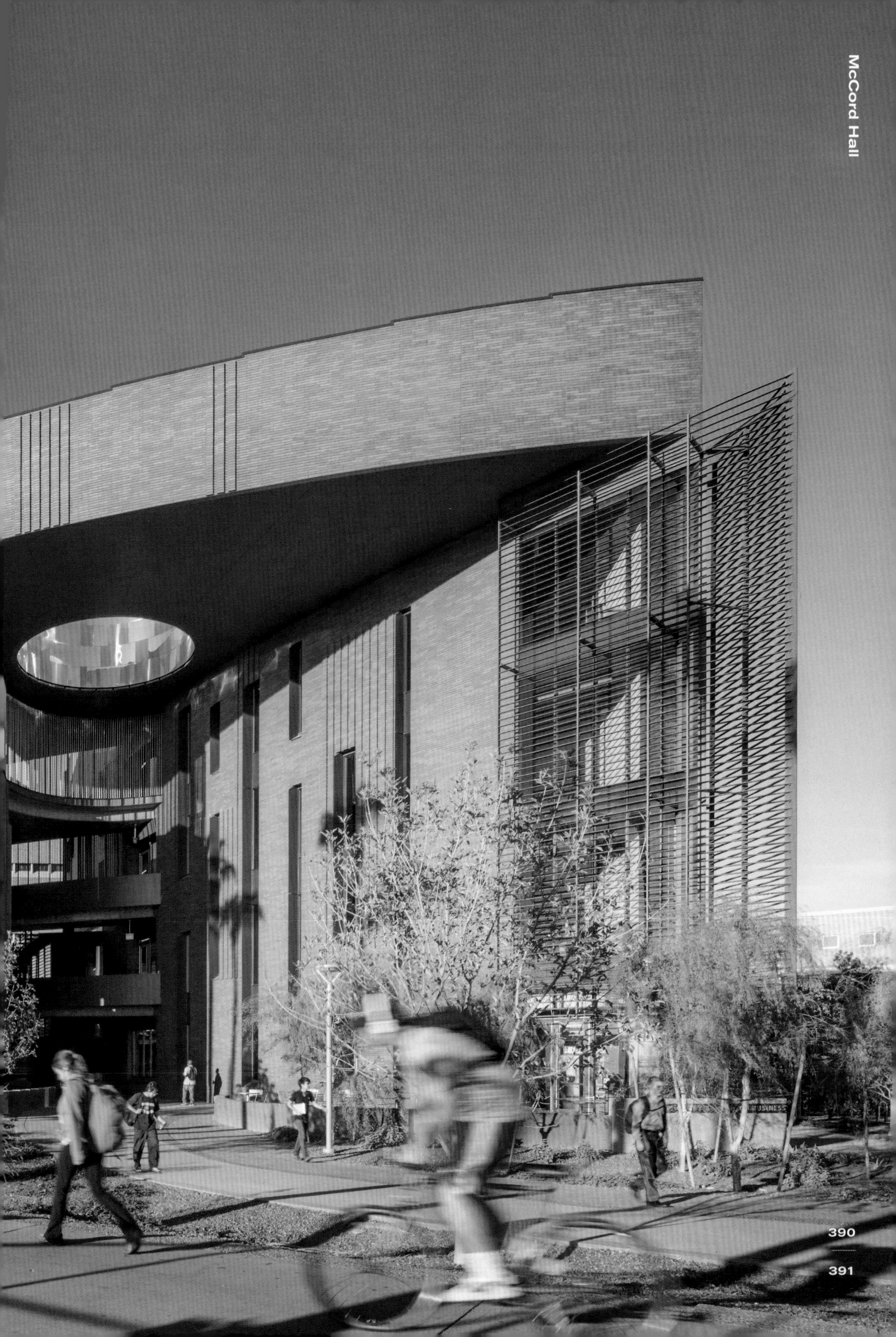
BUSINESS

The Otemachi Tower

Tokyo, Japan — 2014

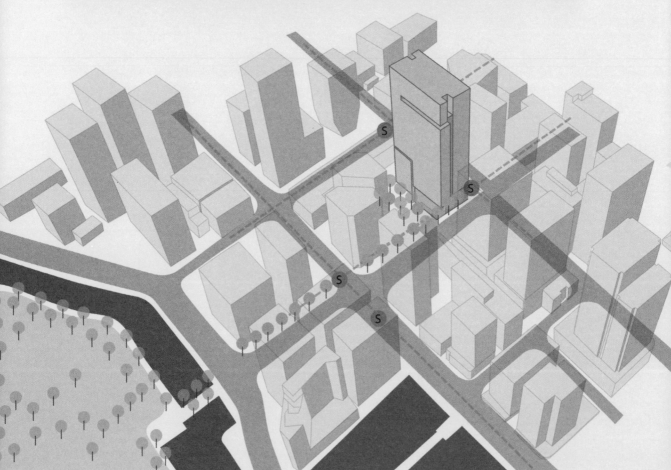

Top: Context plan

The Taisei Corporation, one of Japan's leading contractors, sent a young architect to intern with KPF, each year, for over 25 years. Those young people returned to Japan and eventually rose to levels of leadership in Taisei. Over the years we did several projects in Japan in collaboration with Taisei. We were like relatives. In 2007 they asked us to join them again. They were developing a corporate headquarters for the Mizuho Bank in the Chiyoda Ward of Tokyo. The Imperial Palace and its gardens occupy the largest portion of this ward. The site, to the east of the Palace grounds, and looking into them from high floors, was surrounded by masonry commercial structures of good construction and of sober appearance. Directly connected to the Otemachi Station this location is served by five subway lines. Over 10,000 sq. meters in size, Taisei proposed making one third, 3,600 sq. meters, of the site into an urban forest!

Before initiating the building's design Taisei designed the forest. They selected the French landscape architect, Michel Desvigne, to lead the effort. Eventually 100 species of trees were researched and selected from Japan's mountainous regions to create this unique urban gesture and to generate the bio-diversity they sought as their goal.

Japan always amazed me as a place of enormous contrasts. The most refined cultural accomplishments could exist, cheek by jowl, with the most congested and commercial of urban environments. Still, even in Japan, proposing an urban forest in the heart of Tokyo was an unprecedented, and far-sighted, juxtaposition. We were honored to be given the opportunity to design an architectural response. To us, it suggested one of Zen-like deference.

Our work had been proceeded by a significant amount of preliminary planning already accomplished by Taisei. They had established the structure's volumetric dimensions, its relationship to the proposed forest and its sectional components. Two levels of retail below grade connected directly to passages leading from the Otemachi Station. At grade, a major banking hall for the Mizuho Bank was proposed on the south and a dedicated entry for a hotel on the north. Between these two the upper volume of the retail concourse intervened bringing natural light to the levels below. Escalators from grade led up to the lowest level of the office space. Taisei planned the office floors with an offset core set against the tower's east face, orienting all office views directly toward the Imperial Palace. Finally, terminating the upper levels of the structure, were six floors dedicated to a hotel. All of these components were defined by the enclosure of an elementary rectangular box. Our job was to make architecture of it.

Had it not been for the presence of the adjacent urban forest our response would have been quite different. We would have been inclined to challenge the muteness of the building's shape. Here, however, a restrained architectural presence, verging on silence, seemed necessary in this context. Viewing into the grounds of the Imperial Palace from above and standing next to the quiet voices

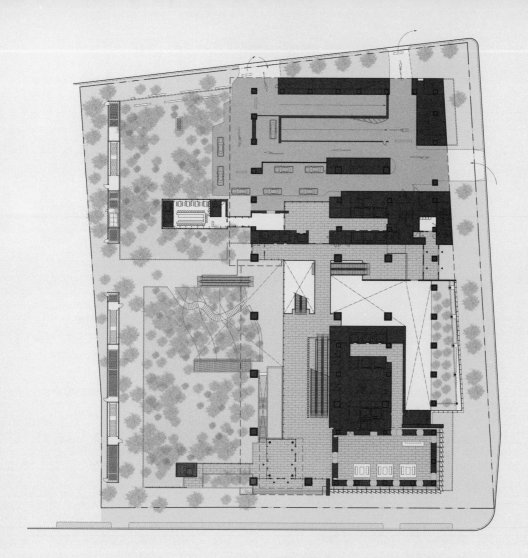

Ground-floor plan

of nature emanating from the forest below inspired a more reserved approach.

We began by searching for a compositional strategy to acknowledge the various programmatic participants of the tower without resorting to an overtly articulated separation of their parts. We were looking for a way of more subtly recognizing them. This search led us to the simulation of interlocking volumes. It was more representational that actual. Functional purists would question our method but we were seeking a means of quietly animating the volume. This led to the horizontal carving out of the mass in recognition of key points of programmatic emphasis. The most dramatic of these excavations occurs on the reception level of the hotel six floors below the highest level of the building. Behind it, on the southwest corner looking to the grounds of the Imperial Palace, reside a swimming pool and the main restaurant of the Aman Resort Hotel which occupies the remainder of the tower above. These horizontal programmatic incisions were then connected with vertical slots carved within the building's surface to create a graphic interplay within the larger surface. The overall interlocking effect of this compositional strategy gave the sense of buildings within a building.

The surface cladding, for this predominately glass structure, is one of its most expressive features. We were looking for a way to give a sense of solidity as well as transparency. This was achievable if substantial vertical projections are introduced on each of the vertical mullions. (Mies van der Rohe did this on the Seagrams Building in New York, to great effect.) By so doing it enables the building, on the oblique, to appear almost solid. This we found to be desirable given the contextual solidity of the masonry buildings surrounding our site.

Our original proposal introduced, on top of the vertical millions, stone fins of 6" in width and 14" in depth. The front surface of the stone fin was to be a rough, fractured, texture giving the building a sense of greater durability. To us this felt right for the building's role as a backdrop to the urban forest. However, fortunately, the weight of the superimposed stone was more than the window wall could bear. Taisei proposed an alternative—cast aluminum. It reduced the weight of each five foot length to only 40 pounds. In cast aluminum the rugged texture of the front face was easily achievable and any metal surface could be simulated. We chose bronze. It was perfect. Like the Seagrams Building it gave a subdued elegance to the structure. It paired perfectly with the forest below and with the surrounding masonry structures. Developing the wall further we decided to introduce a horizontal emphasis. This enhanced the scale of the wall. We achieved this by separating the vertical fins every third floor. At this juncture we wove horizontal metal bands between them.

On the lower levels the vertical texture, created by the projecting bronze fins, was transformed into vertical elements structural glass. Individual rhythms created in the spacing of the glass structural fins were developed to articulate the presence of unique programmatic

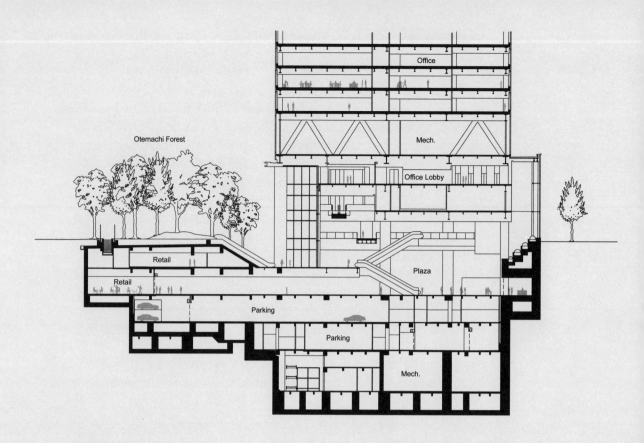

Otemachi Forest

Office

Mech.

Office Lobby

Plaza

Retail

Retail

Parking

Parking

Mech.

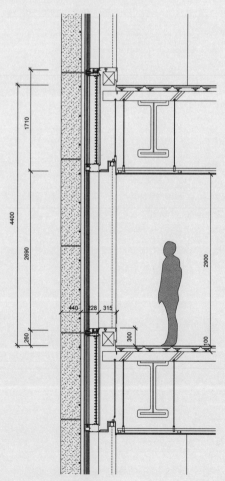

1710

4400

2690

2900

440 228 315

300

260

1100

Top: Longitudinal section

elements at the ground levels. Of these, enclosure of the banking hall, on the southeast corner, is the most dramatic. Behind the glass stone clad piers are layered to give the room a powerful and protected sense in its prominent urban position.

We are Western architects. When we talk of giving a Japanese sensibility to the character of a building, it has to be met with some skepticism. But our intent was to do a building which felt totally at home in Tokyo and, more specifically, in this part of Tokyo. Subsequent to developing the external character of the building we set about developing the major interior spaces with the same intention. Here we introduced numerous vertically striated surfaces of wood, metal and stone. These we thought to be representative of the esthetic we sought. Restrained warmth and elegance were our goals. So too, were they the goals for Kerry Hill, the interior architects of the Aman Resort Hotel. As a result the entire building speaks with a single esthetic voice. It is a voice inspired by a restrained esthetic interacting with nature. This, we viewed as the bond which formed the essence of the Japanese artistic sensibility.

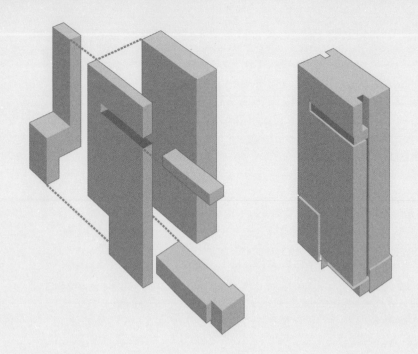

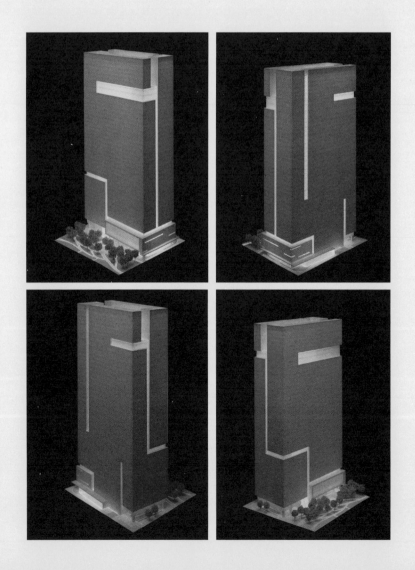

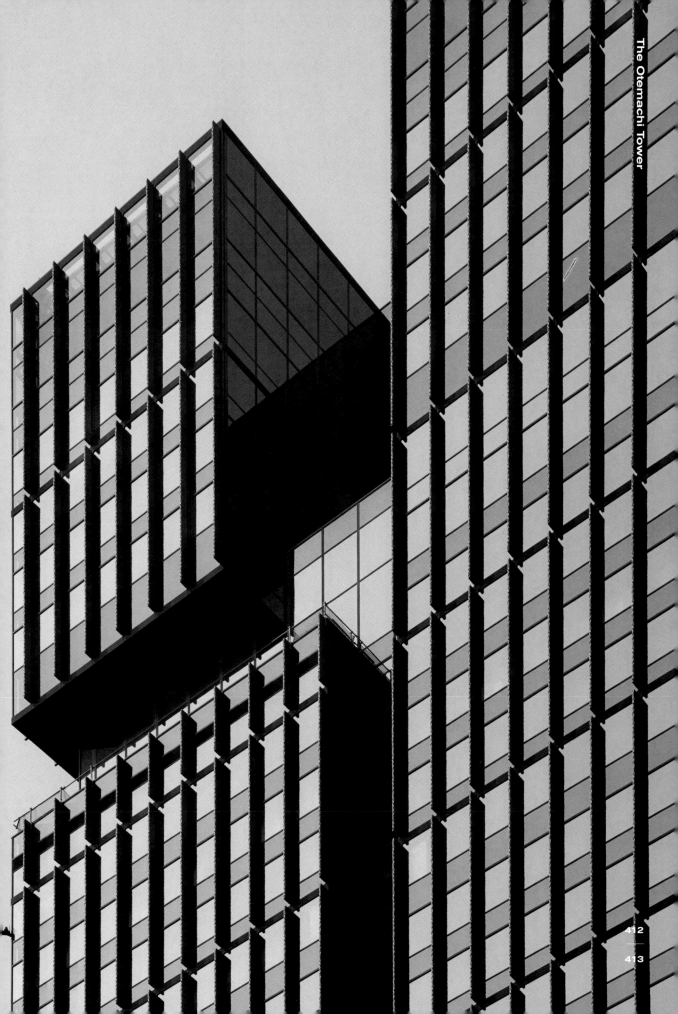

Advanced Science Research Center

City University of New York,
New York, U.S. — 2015

On the basis of the "Vertical Campus" at Baruch College, which I designed in the early 1990s, its president, Dr. Matthew Goldstein, commissioned KPF as architects of the Advanced Science Research Center for the City College of New York in 2003, after he became the chancellor of the City University of New York.

We were honored. The City College of New York is a storied institution. For years, during the middle of the 20th century, it was called the "poor man's Harvard." Founded before the Civil War, it was intended to provide a free education for the immigrants who were flooding the city. It succeeded brilliantly. Ten Nobel Prize winners in science have come from its ranks, along with many of America's most prominent cultural figures. Graduates include Jonas Salk, Woody Allen, Henry Kissinger, Bernard Baruch, Colin Powell, Felix Frankfurter, Upton Sinclair, and Ira Gershwin. Dr. Goldstein himself was one of its graduates.

Located in the upper reaches of Manhattan between 130th and 141st streets, it caps the ridge of St. Nicholas Park, one of the highest points in Manhattan. Historically the site occupied the northern end of an old Indigenous American footpath that continued down a long crest through Manhattan to the southern tip of the island. During the War of Independence, revolutionary forces chose the location for a strategically located encampment.

History aside, the site is one of the most singular in the city. Located on high land at the narrowest part of the island where the Harlem River branches off from the Hudson, its north-south grain follows the primary axis of Manhattan. Here, the site is a short land passage between the two rivers; conversely, as a peninsula, it allows passage by water between rivers around its northern shoreline. This north-south flow, whether by land or water, informed our architectural response, inspiring us to use architecture to enhance the meaning of the site.

Built for scientific research, the full complex will eventually contain three structures. The first phase, now complete, is composed of two structures: the Advanced Science Research Center (ASRC), and the City College Center for Discovery and Innovation. We designed each with a distinct physical strategy adapted to its own methods of pursuing scientific objectives.

The ASRC building is arranged thematically on five floors dedicated to five areas of research: Photonics, Structural Biology, Remote Sensing, Nanotechnology, and Neuroscience. In contrast, the City College Center for Discovery and Innovation houses multiple disciplines on each floor, encouraging interdisciplinary work on joint topics and projects. The intention of both buildings is to promote active collaboration among researchers.

The programmatic composition of both buildings required two fundamentally different types of space: spaces for experimentation and research (labs) and spaces for private study and group discussion (offices and conference rooms). We created a third type of space—lounges, vertical circulation nodes, an auditorium, and a cafeteria—as the glue binding the first two. We joined the two buildings below grade with a vivarium and facilities for imagining

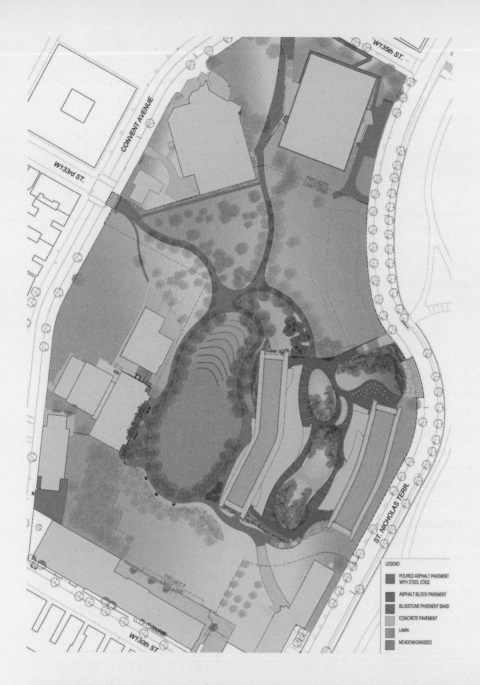

LEGEND

POURED ASPHALT PAVEMENT
WITH STEEL EDGE

ASPHALT BLOCK PAVEMENT

BLUESTONE PAVEMENT BAND

CONCRETE PAVEMENT

LAWN

MEADOW/GRASSES

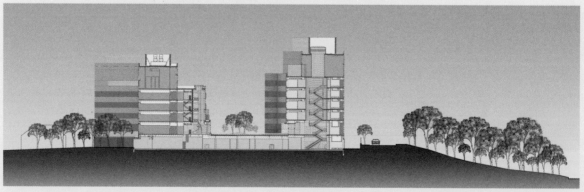

Campus site plan, longitudinal section

modalities, behavioral studies and cryophysics. Loading and maintenance areas are located below grade.

Of the two fundamental types of space, laboratories are the most dimensionally driven, and they form the backbone of these structures. However, their configurations continually change to serve different kinds of experiments. Modular construction was necessary to facilitate flexible arrangements.

Early in the design process, we found that a 60' laboratory width composed of two 30' structural bays was optimal, and that each building should provide two labs on each floor, inflected where each met the vertical transportation. We laminated a circulation zone 10' wide on each side of the labs, the outer zone serving the labs and the inner zone, the private offices and conference areas. We book-ended either end of the laboratory blocks with conference spaces.

In contrast to the necessary orthogonal geometry of the laboratories, the second zone, for private offices and conference areas, could be more fluid and dynamic spatially. The juxtaposition of curved and rectangular geometries was the basis of the buildings' expression.

Placed opposite each other, the length of the two facing lab structures created a framed outdoor public passage between the opposing façades. We then had the choice of facing the offices, conference rooms, and such ancillary facilities as the coffee shop out to the views of Manhattan, or to orient them inward, toward each other. We chose the latter in order to generate a greater sense of intimacy in the public outdoor space, and to foster a sense of communication between the two scientific communities.

With the strong suggestion of movement heading downstream between the two buildings, we developed the buildings metaphorically as the steep, stepped banks of a river channel. Cultivating the sense of dynamic flow made the space feel more experiential and immersive, and therefore more participatory and human. To enhance the geological dynamism, we striated projecting glass mullions vertically across the façades, spacing them closely to accentuate the curvature of the walls. The close spacing generated narrow sections of flat glass that increased the façades' sense of movement. We extended fins of fritted glass from each of the mullions, which shaded the façades while allowing transparency. The chamfered outer edges of the fins fracture sunlight into rainbows that project inside. (We had done this on our Gannett building many years before.) The fins also enhanced the feeling of the wall's fluidity by adding a predominately horizontal flow laid over the vertical scoring.

Landscaping enhanced the spatial fluidity of this public space, and it added intimacy. Since the space, bracketed by glass cliffs on either side, was already flowing like a river, we reinforced the analogy to nature by landscaping islands of greenery within the flow of the river. The islands took the shape of curvilinear, somewhat elliptical, interlocking mounds of wild grasses that created room-like passages between them.

The spatial sequence of streaming water comes to a head at the entrance of the two structures. Just beyond the front door, a vertical

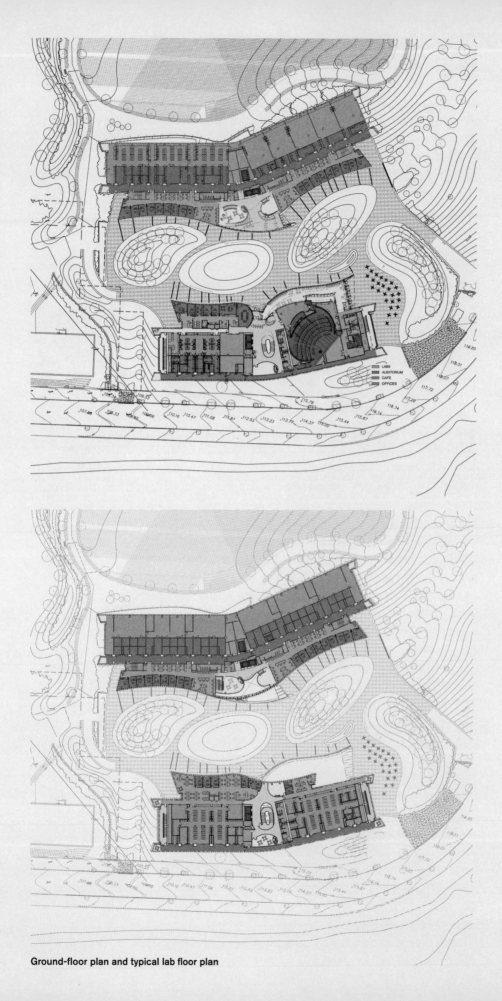

Ground-floor plan and typical lab floor plan

atrium soars the full height of the building, revealing the building's section. We populated the intersection of each floor and the atrium with social spaces designed to stimulate spontaneous gathering and an awareness of the buildings' collaborative scientific community. Each of these spaces has a personality distinct from the adjacent labs, and they are unabashedly playful, colorful, and evocative. Various types of dichroic glass splash stair balustrades with colors that change as they transmit variations in natural light.

In the context of the city, the paired buildings crown the highest point in northern Manhattan, St. Nicholas Terrace. Their north-south axis reinforces Manhattan's dominant thrust. The buildings acknowledge and respect the urban character of the site. But in addition, we used nature as an aspirational metaphor to stimulate the imaginations of students and researchers who, at the forward edge of scientific exploration, are pursuing what is not yet known. The building, like the scientists, is pushing limits.

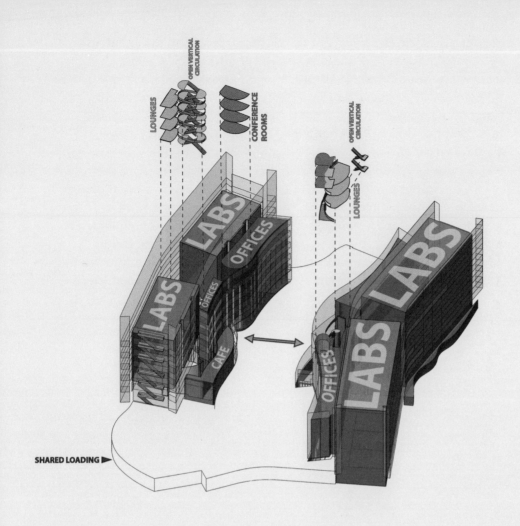

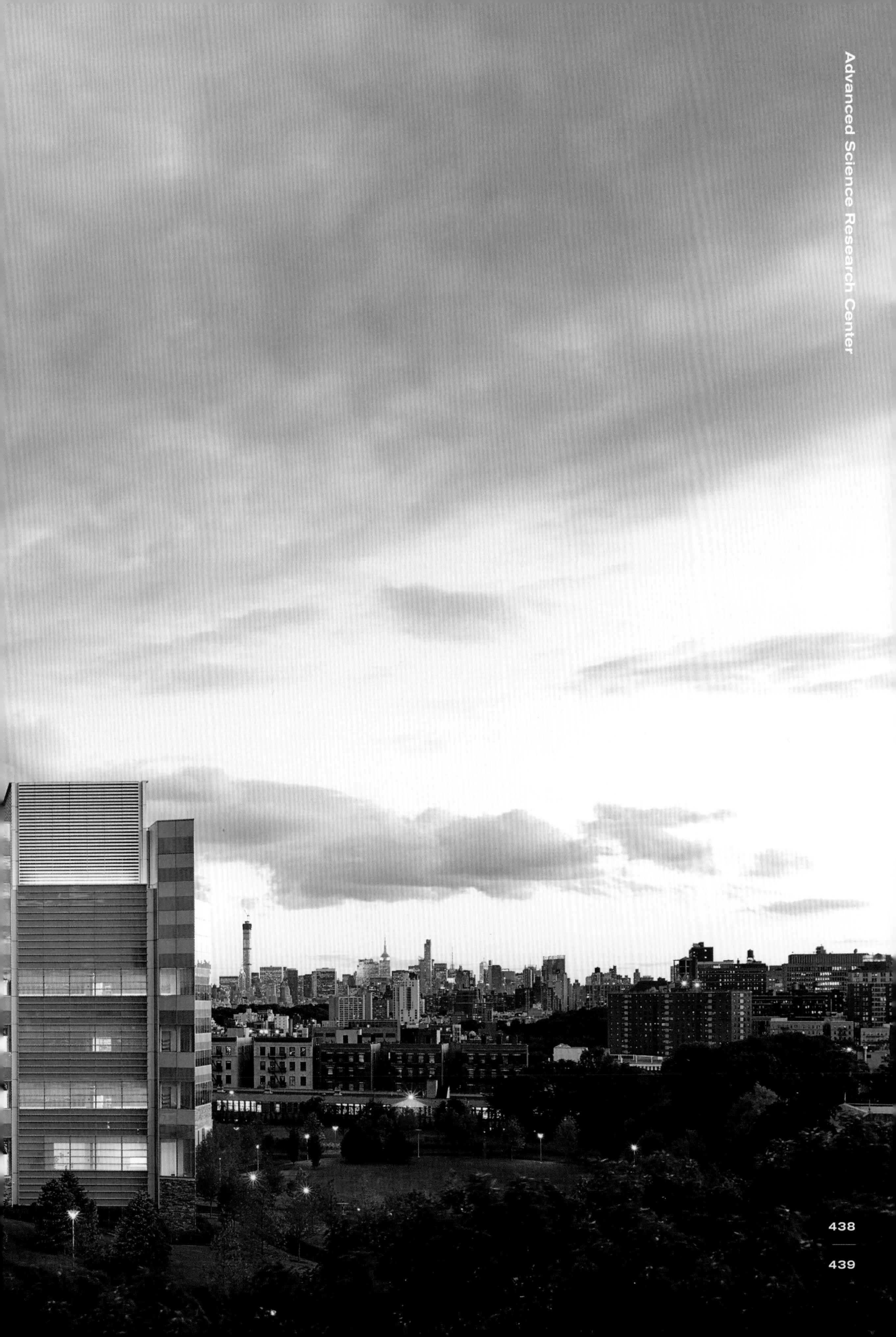

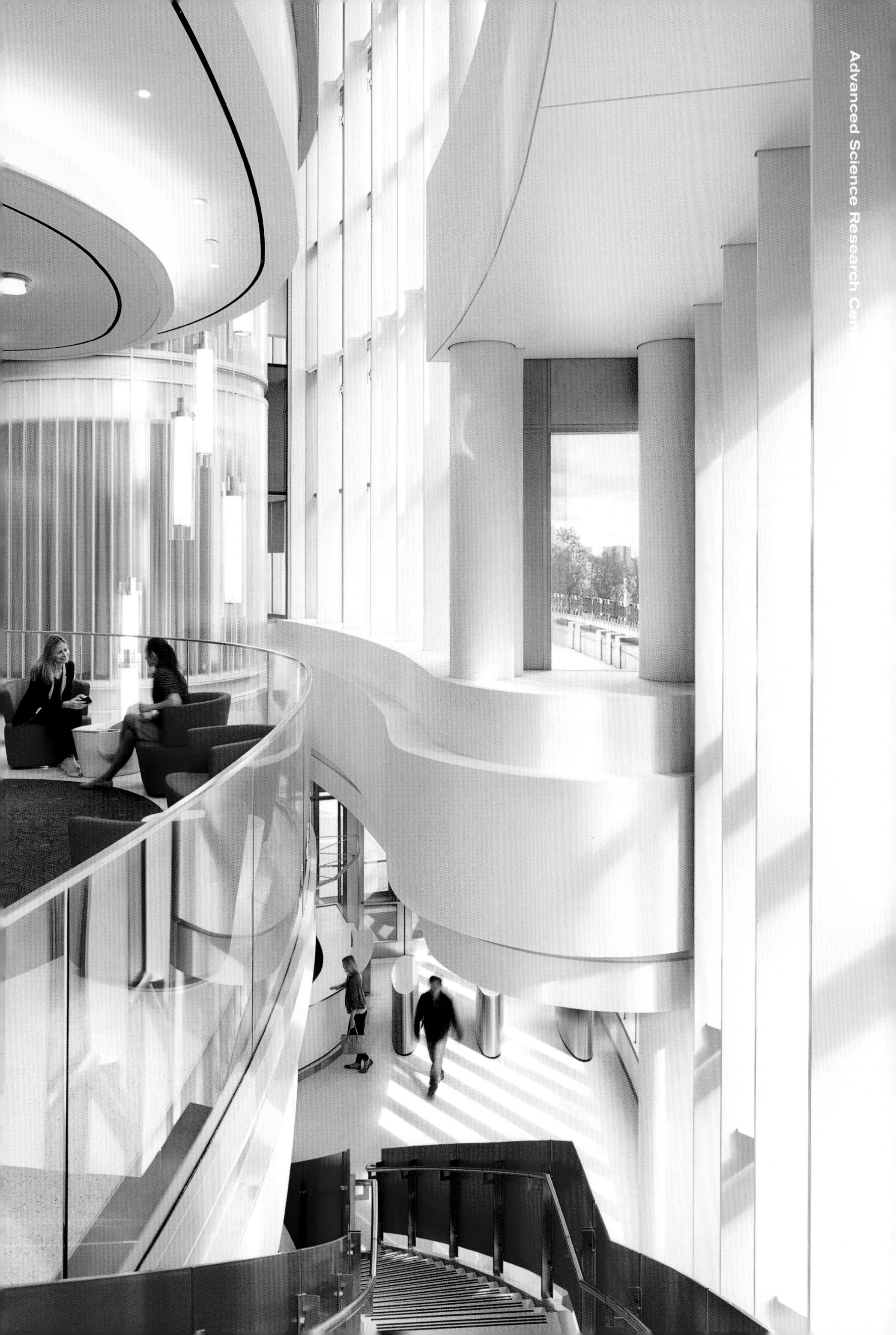

Ross School
of Business

University of Michigan, Ann Arbor, U.S.
2009 phase 1 — 2017 phase 2

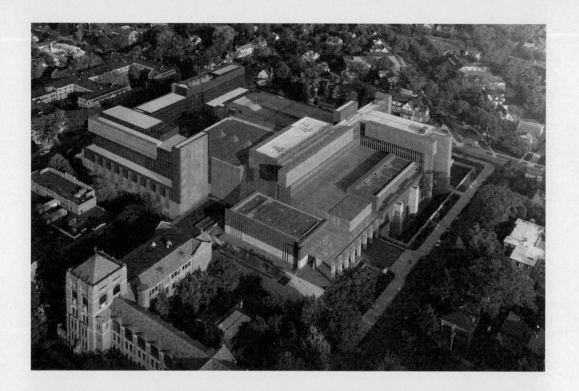

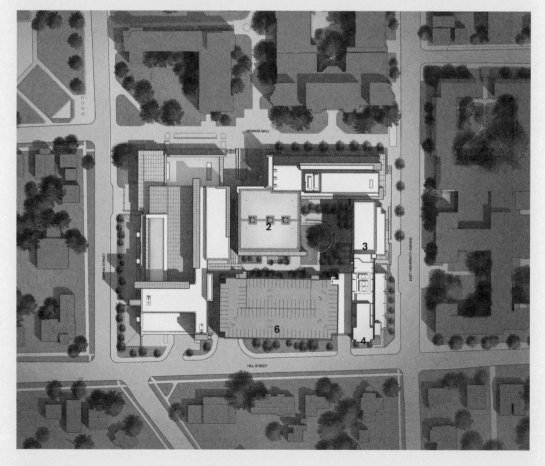

Site plan

1. Blau Hall (2016)
2. Kresge Hall (Renovated/Reclad 2016)
3. Exec. Res. (Overclad/Reclad 2016–2018)
4. Wyly Hall (Overclad/Reclad 2016–2018)
5. Alessi Courtyard
6. Parking Garage (Overclad/Screen Wall)

The scope of our 2003 commission for redesigning the Ross School of Business at the University of Michigan was originally modest, simply a matter of replanning and reorganizing the school within its existing complex of buildings. Dean Robert Dolan had recognized serious functional inadequacies in its physical organization that impeded his aspirations to develop leaders of the global economy. He wanted to lift the impediments.

But our early studies revealed that nothing short of a new facility would solve the problems, a position that was seconded by New York developer Stephen M. Ross, when the highly successful graduate of the school saw the architectural possibilities. Mr. Ross, a business leader of the type the school aspires to shape and nurture, offered to finance most of the new construction.

The 12 years of construction was done in two phases, and the project eventually came to occupy nearly its full campus block. The school managed to continue operations without interruption during the 12 years.

Our structuring concept was to create a great room within which all the functions of the school would converge—a place of constant activity that would hum like a beehive. Our strategy in buildings of this type is to build a strong sense of community through physical design, and in the Ross school, we strived to achieve community by designing a room that stimulated social interaction while establishing an environment for study. Learning the skills of social interaction was as much a part of the Dean Dolan's vision for the school as were his other pedagogical objectives. The school's mission is based in a working method of collaborative interaction the school calls "action learning," with which we happened to feel great affinity. The attitude paralleled our own process of collaborative and comparative design.

Acoustics, natural light, human scale, and a sense of warmth were important drivers in making this kind of space: every physical and psychological aspect of a room like this matters. So do the functions of the room and the adjacent spaces. We placed the cafeteria prominently so that at any time of day coffee is available, along with breakfast, lunch, and dinner at mealtimes. Students gravitate to this room whenever they are not in class. A beautiful 5,000-square-foot carpet, specially designed for the space, lies under the tables, absorbing sound and lending the room a feeling of serenity. The circularity of the tables encourages team conversation. Three-story columns supporting the glass skylight populate the edges of the tall, three-story space forming a peristyle hall bounded by majestic colonnades running down the middle of the long space. Mirroring devises deflect and distribute light evenly.

We positioned a three-floor stack of tiered 85-person classrooms at one side of the room, each floor equipped with four classrooms. With the middle floor on the same level as the main floor of the great space, students only have to walk a level up or down, a strategy that lightens the elevator load and encourages social interaction on the stairs. Each classroom has glass-fronted study rooms for six-person team interaction facing the main space.

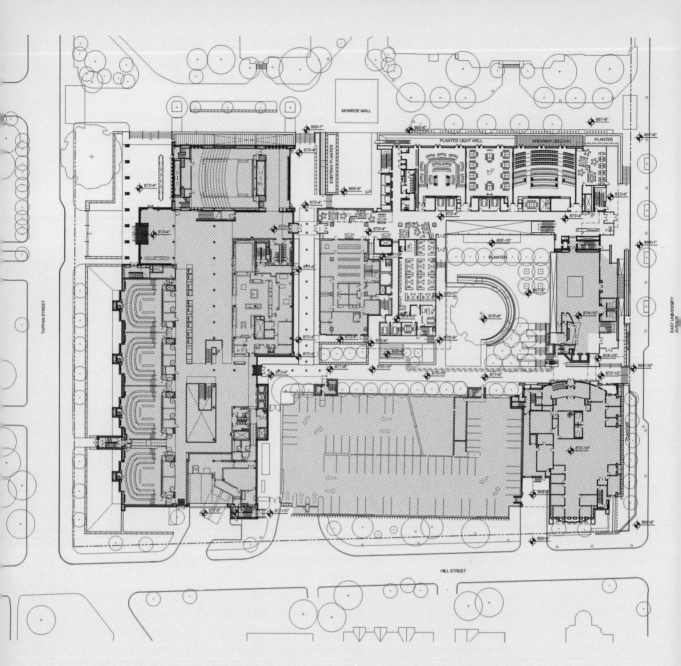

Ground-floor plan

A two-tiered auditorium for 500 people forms a third wall of the space, and administrative offices above the cafeteria and a lower study area complete its enclosure. Faculty offices and the dean's suite are located above the study areas, under the skylight. Additional faculty offices and special spaces for the faculty lounge and for colloquia partially reside in a glazed cantilevered horizontal volume outside, above the atrium's skylight.

At almost any time of day or night the long, tall study/dining hall is filled with teams of students studying and talking together in many units of collaboration. The space gathers almost all of the school's community. Completed in the first phase of construction it continued to be the school's center of activity when we joined it to the second, and final phase of construction.

At the south end of the University's traditional stone-and-brick campus quadrangle, diagonally opposite the gothic-style law school, the solid materiality of the nearby traditional buildings demanded an equivalent material. Our dominant cladding is terra cotta, rich in color and solid in feeling: it equals the neighboring buildings in physical presence. Vertically striated, the broad expanses of terra cotta walls part to make space for ribbed fenestration in the office areas while closing to the full opacity of a masonry wall when fenestration is not desired. However, the terra cotta walls never meet the ground, and rest instead on a warm limestone base that seems to lift the terra cotta and suspend gravity. The textured limestone gives a crafted, tactile sense at the height of the passing human body.

Long glazed cantilevered glass-enclosed tubes of space are the most dramatic of the façade elements. Some are vertical, enclosing stairs projecting from the building's mass, and others are horizontal, enclosing special spaces on the upper floors of the structure. Together the juxtaposition of the horizontal and vertical becomes the school's dominant visual element. Their geometric drama is exceeded only by the stone-colonnaded entrance portico that looks and acts as an open trellis filtering light. It's one of the many outdoor zones that we created throughout the complex. Cantilevering beyond stone-clad columns, its fully glazed roof interlocks with a tall volume of glass that encloses the atrium. Pyramidal skylights under the entry canopy, at grade, bring natural light down to the exercise spaces below.

The success of the first phase encouraged Mr. Ross to finance the remainder of the school's campus in a second phase. With the instincts of a developer who sees the whole, he wanted to tie it all together into an integrated complex. Though mostly new construction, this second phase included the re-cladding of three existing buildings and an existing parking structure. Unexpectedly, the re-cladding presented a great challenge. Physical limitations of the existing structures resisted the re-cladding selected in the first phase, and finally, for financial reasons, we retained the existing weather enclosures while superposing a terra cotta screen of vertical ribs and narrow glass elements. The cladding was the most difficult challenge of the second phase, but, in the end, the solution

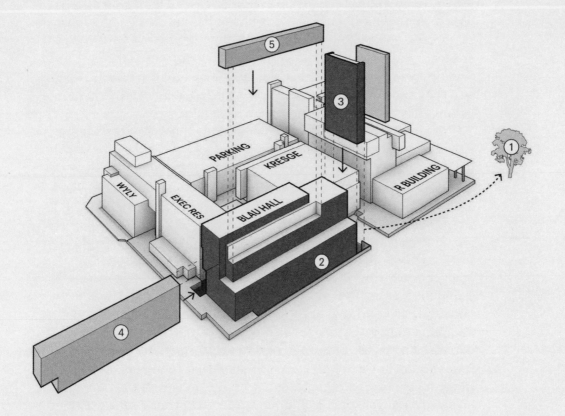

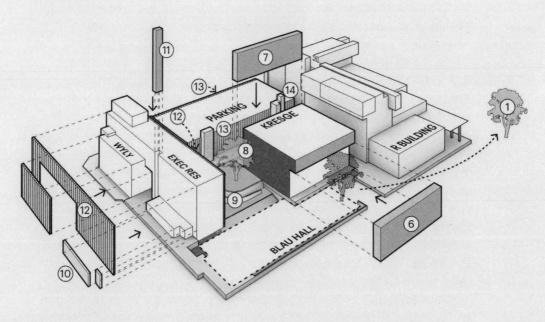

1. Relocate tree
2. Building Blau Hall
3. Insert core
4. Insert atrium
5. Insert special piece
6. Insert Kresge atrium
7. Insert Kresge glass volume
8. Preserve tree
9. Drop level of courtyard
10. Change Wyly lobby
11. Add Wyly glass piece
12. Add garage screen wall
13. Clad elevator towers

of providing a second layer proved to be one of the design's most successful features.

The existing Kresge Library, which bifurcated the business school campus, seemed to prevent joining the two parts. We found that by surrounding the building with public courtyards we could integrate its mass and transform its presence strategically from an obstacle to a pivot hinging the two phases. We created one courtyard at the termination of a campus axis, where we glazed a façade of the library, and positioning student lounges directly behind the glass wall. On the opposite side of Kresge where there was an existing courtyard we clad the façade in ribbed terra cotta to warm and honor the public space, and give the space greater architectural value. On a third façade, we used glass to create another outdoor zone, defining a relatively narrow passage between the library and the parking structure to the south. A glass roof plane projects out into the courtyard, animating the space with its visual thrust.

The second phase of construction was completed on a zone of the site previously occupied by three buildings. Two were retained, but demolishing the third liberated a generous bar of space for a new classroom structure. We capped one end with a glass volume revealing elevators and a stair, and the movement continuously activates the side of the courtyard between the two construction phases. As in phase one, we created a special gathering room, boxing it in a horizontal tube of glass cantilevered out from its supporting terra cotta volume. In the second phase, we elaborated on the language of interlocking cubic brick-and-glass volumes and planes that we had developed in the first phase. The overall composition is complex and porous, as though puzzled together.

In the final leg of the complex along one of the campus's main arteries, East University Avenue, we introduced a prominent street entry that initiates an axis-joining phase two to phase one. We animated the walk along this important line of movement with a series of study lounges, which we glazed to enhance the public and social nature of the space. One lounge faces an existing south-facing courtyard, which we landscaped and humanized with grade changes and stone retaining walls. The other lounge faces north to another courtyard. This linear zone of space, devoted to team study areas, acts as a spatial corollary to the socializing function of the great room in phase two. Together they are cores that sponsor the life of the building.

The remaining functions in existing buildings along East University Avenue are predominately programmed as hotel rooms used for executive education and dining functions. Recladding their surfaces in terra cotta and glass brought them into a balanced relationship with the new phases of construction—into the integrated whole that Mr. Ross wanted.

The project was completed after 15 years of continuous construction. Fortunately, the school had a long attention span, but finally the support for the design and the patience during the long two phases yielded a building that cultivates a vibrant activity that gives the school its feeling of motivation and purpose. Given the quality of the materials and detailing afforded by Mr. Ross's generosity, all at the service of an intriguing spatial complexity, the complex honors its neighboring brick-and-stone antecedents. Built to last like those older structures, the level of quality is rarely seen in modern academic construction.

Architecture can shape an institution. Judging by the collective spirit evident to anyone stepping into its halls, the design has been transformative, embodying the school's belief in collaborative interaction and action learning.

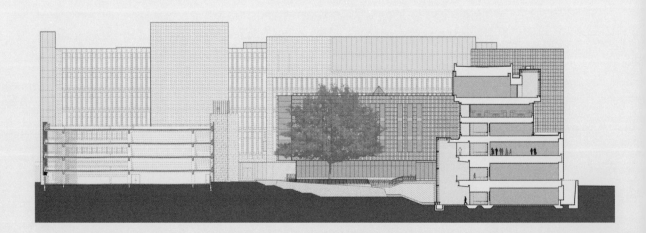

Longitudinal section

Samuel Zell &
Robert H. Lurie Institute
for Entrepreneurial Studies

52 Lime Street

London, U.K. — 2018

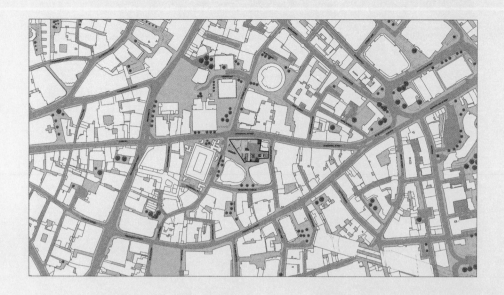

Context and ground floor plan

Introducing tall buildings into the historic center of the City of London always generates controversy, yet admitting new arrivals that shoulder their way into the pack is necessary and almost inevitable in a modern, progressive, urban environment, even when it is already dense. London's town planners recognized this dilemma, and facing the controversy and the relentless pressure to build to ever-greater heights, they elected to cluster tall buildings together into a type of pyramidal massing created by their collective form. The intention was to have buildings, each with a strong personality, that build to an architectural crescendo.

The buildings that form the base of the crescendo are now in place, awaiting the final structure that will mark the cluster's conclusion against the sky. Each is a strong statement in itself and speaks to the other with energy and respect.

What has already been created, in effect, is a type of urban drama. Every participant in the play has been shaped by the necessity of respecting view corridors to St. Paul's Cathedral. Each does it uniquely, but collectively they form an architectural dialogue. The first to be constructed was the "Gherkin," perhaps the most insular and self-contained of the group. Its dramatic form triggered like responses. Next came the "Cheesegrater," which was our nearest neighbor. Its sloping front façade leans back to respect the view corridor.

Given the highly textural structures adjacent to ours, we chose to design their foil, which responds with mirrored surfaces and formal gestures that makes for an exceptional architectural conversation and heightened urban theater.

The surrounding buildings are, texturally, rough. Ours is smooth, and reflective. All these existing structures in this tight context represent different eras in history, most venerable being the St. Andrew Undershaft Church, directly across from us on Leadenhall Street. The façade of our structure mirrors St. Andrew. Lloyd's of London, also an immediate neighbor, is clad in a textured surface of a more aggressive order. Our mirrored structure mirrors Lloyd's, a foil that accepts its context.

Origami was the impetus for the form of our tower on Lime Street. As the building rises, it folds back to angle to a point on the sky. Affectionately dubbed the "Scalpel," it enthusiastically joins its unique neighbors by virtue of its own uniqueness. Never have we had the opportunity to add one of our tall buildings to such a rich and dramatic context, as though participating in a contemporary version of the imaginary vistas of specimen buildings that Renaissance architects called veduta.

The compacted quality of this dense part of London creates an unusual if not unique urban experience generated by the fact that it is not regulated by a normal street grid. Every building site here has a unique geometry. Everything is squeezed together. My comparison of unique collections of disparate buildings to an urban cocktail party is more apt here than anywhere else where we have built. Because all the participants are so densely packed and juxtaposed, their idiosyncratic differences bring them together more than if they were consciously trying to relate.

Clockwise from upper left: north, south, east, and west elevations

This inchoate context is the environment within which Richard Rogers first introduced his Lloyd's of London building. He responded by pulling out from the body of the building all of its insides. Nothing could have been less "contextual." Surprisingly it works, wonderfully so. Lloyd's is a near neighbor as is his latest addition, the Cheesegrater. Both buildings are highly textural but not contextual.

When we started working with this site, we explored options using our "comparative method," looking for a gesture that responded appropriately to this architecturally intense, competitive place. Nothing seemed to work. It was not until we tried folding volumes inward rather than outward with angled planes that the building seemed to feel right in its spot within this context. Leaning inward is natural for a skyscraper but the inclination resonated with its neighbors, Foster's Gherkin and Rogers's Cheesegrater, which both lean inward and taper to a more slender top. The Scalpel and Rogers's Cheesegrater are on opposite sides of Leadenhall Street, which leads directly to St. Paul's. Together the buildings frame the view corridor to the Cathedral.

While the origami concluded in the sky, it started at the street before ascending the shaft. Three steps informed its faceted massing. The first step was to rotate the west wall of our volume off from the alignment of Lime Street to create a triangular plaza in front of the Willis building: that building needed breathing space so we created an intimate urban room. Our second step was to generate a transition between our tower and the adjacent structure to the west along Leadenhall Street. To accomplish this we made the upper portion of our Leadenhall-facing façade narrower by turning it before it reached the neighboring building. The turn generated a transitional moment that linked the tower to its neighbor. The third step was to create a fold on the Leadenhall façade. It began at the height of our western neighbor and ascended to the building's highest point before plunging to the intersection of Lime and Leadenhall, the building's touchdown.

The triangular geometry of this fold initiated the larger triangulation of the remainder of the north façade as it leaned back from Leadenhall. The resulting triangular gesture acknowledged the geometry of the Cheesegrater opposite. The eastern edge of this rotated triangular surface emerges as the building's salient edge and dominant marker. It's a reverse thunderbolt originating at the ground and racing to the sky.

We kept the building's geometry clear with minimalist cladding. To heighten the folds and their sense of movement across the planes of the tower, we quieted the triple-glazed curtain wall (required for energy savings) by reducing the number of mullions, sublimating their profiles into the glazing. The glass panels were a full floor in height and 1.5 meters in width, and the exceptional size resulted in a flatness that brought out the folding. The planes did not want any surface differentiations such as dimensional or directional shifts or changes in curtain wall type such as shingling.

We carried the simplicity of the building's texture into the interior. Smooth flat planes of travertine give mass to the building's interior spaces. Handrails are incised into the stone balustrades of the stairs to emphasize the solidity and planarity of the walls. If the exterior is

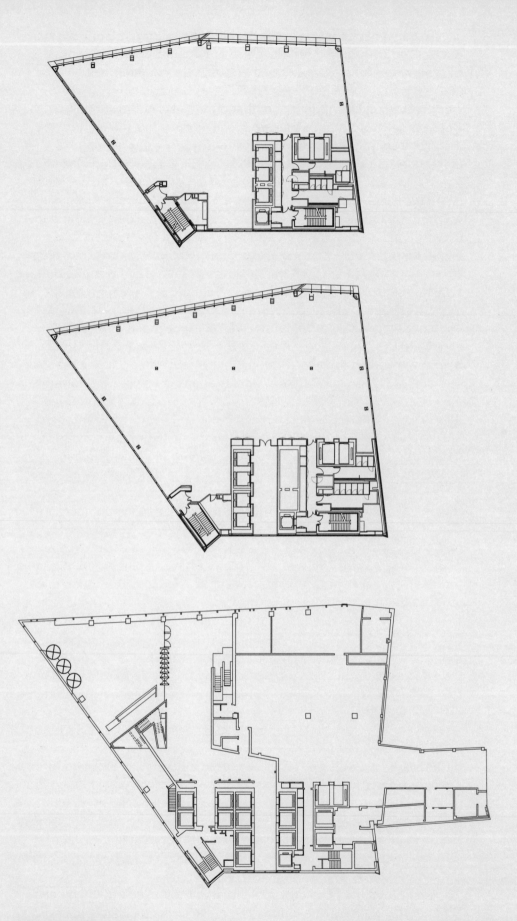

Typical high-rise floorplan
Typical mid-rise floorplan
Ground floorplan

as weightless as possible, the interior is as weighty as possible. We dramatized the lengthy promenade from the entry to the elevators with multiple layers of ascending volumes accentuating the verticality of the passage. Taking the elevators from the entry promenade, visitors land on individual floors that offer views out toward the city. The geometry allowed by placing the core on an outside wall opened unusual view opportunities, even from exterior egress stairs.

Cultivating a tall building's "objectness" has never been a goal in my work. On the contrary, I have tried to diminish the formal independence of a tall building. But 52 Lime Street was different. It was the smallest in this cluster of formally ambitious buildings and it had to survive the intense architectural competition. To take part in this ensemble with commensurate stature, without being deferential, we had to meet and match their uniqueness with our own. In a way it was like going to a costume party. If you weren't exceptional you didn't fit in. We wanted to fit in, so we were exceptional too.

Curiously, the value I place in having participated in this design experience lies in the degree to which it challenged ideals that I have held sacred. The lesson I learned was the need to accept a humility that allows me to deal with each individual situation on its own terms.

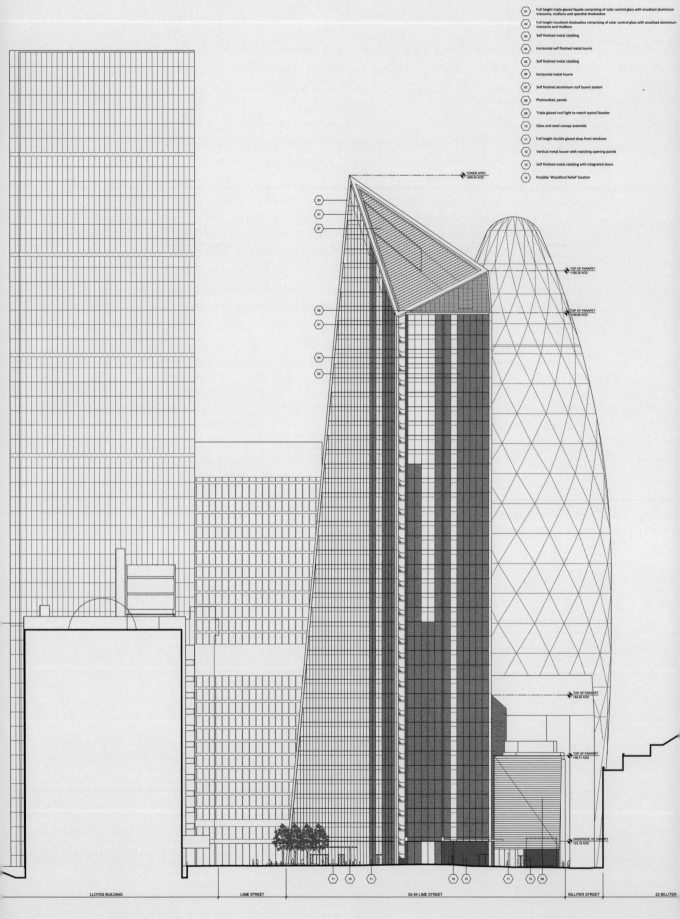

TOWER APEX
+206.50 AOD

TOP OF PARAPET
+180.28 AOD

TOP OF PARAPET
+168.88 AOD

TOP OF PARAPET
+83.40 AOD

TOP OF PARAPET
+46.71 AOD

UNDERSIDE OF CANOPY
+23.18 AOD

LLOYDS BUILDING   LIME STREET   52-54 LIME STREET   BILLITER STREET   22 BILLITER

0   10

South elevation with context

Hudson Yards

New York City, New York, U.S. – 2019

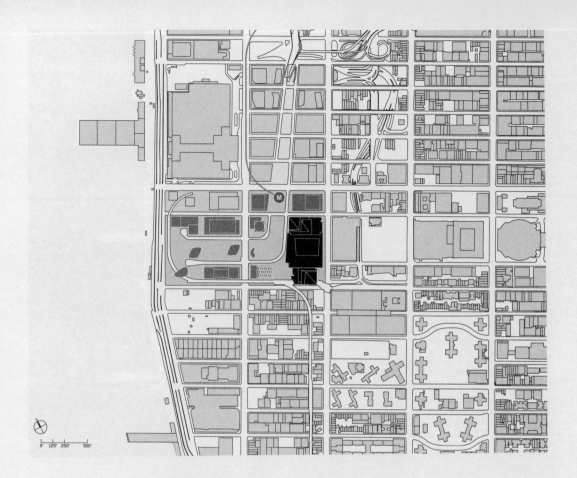

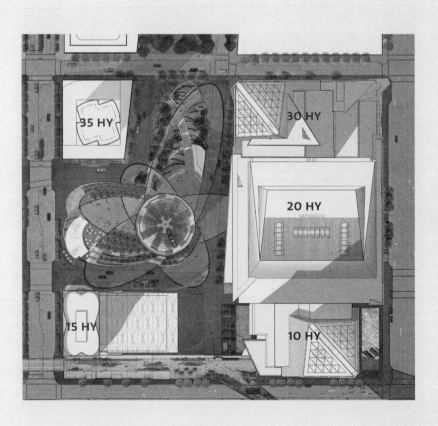

35 HY

30 HY

20 HY

15 HY

10 HY

Context and Plaza plans

Throughout my career I have explored ways to socialize buildings of great size within the surrounding city so that they participate with neighboring structures to cultivate an urban life. By their self-contained nature, tall buildings stand aloof, either unwilling or unable to engage in urban conversation. For me, our commission to design very-tall buildings at Hudson Yards was an opportunity to test and prove at large scale my long-held philosophy of "gesture and response." Toward the end of my long career, it was a final exam, all the more eventful because we were not designing one building but two, along with a third retail component nested in between.

To start the architectural conversation with nearby buildings, however, we initiated the conversation within our own project: the two towers themselves would gesture and respond to each other through movement, as in a dance. It would be our architectural version of *Westside Story*.

The point of departure was, as always, the program. Our client, The Related Companies, wanted the office towers to be the most efficient in New York. Attracting tenants to this then-remote site required both economical rents and highly usable space. Among all the buildings in Hudson Yards, ours would be the tallest; and, positioned the farthest east, along Tenth Avenue, they would be prominent lead structures that introduced the whole project. They had the responsibility of representing the larger project and even performing as its architectural logos. If successful, they could be iconic.

The planning of commercial structures in New York's real-estate market depends on dimensions. Developers believe the most efficient office floor is 45 from the building's core to the outside wall. Ideally, this dimension is maintained throughout the entire height of the structure, but the core of a tall building—with its elevators, bathrooms, stairs, and duct shafts—varies. Elevator banks, each serving 15 floors, drop off one by one along the side of the core as fewer people rise to the higher floors. The rectangular volume of the core steps back and forms a segmented slope on one side. If the 45-foot dimension of office space is to be maintained throughout the height of the building, the corresponding side of the building envelope needs to slope too.

We designed one façade of each tower following the slope of the core. What seemed to be a formal design move was actually based on a very practical consideration. This highly pragmatic decision informed every design response that followed. We developed the diagonal line and its corollary, the oblique plane throughout the complex: visual dynamism became its signature.

Given an angled façade on each tower, our second step was to face the sloping façade of both towers in opposing directions. We oriented the sloping side of the smaller southern tower west toward the Hudson River, and the northern tower toward its neighbor in the sky, the Empire State Building, several blocks east, so they could converse eye to eye at their great altitudes. Their scale and proximity within several blocks offered the possibility of a further conversation as we continued to devise other gestures that would magnify their cross-town chat.

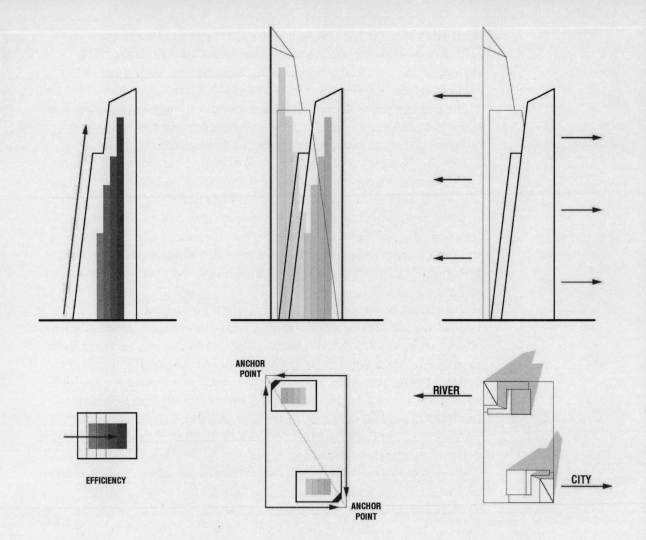

EFFICIENCY

ANCHOR
POINT

ANCHOR
POINT

RIVER

CITY

Facing our two towers in opposite directions generated an unusual energy between them. We extended that dynamic engagement in subsequent design decisions that targeted the immediate context.

The south tower's immediate surroundings were very different from that of the north tower, especially because of its adjacency to the High Line. This elevated train track, which once serviced the Meatpacking District on Manhattan's Westside, was restored as a linear urban park, and quickly became one of New York's most popular tourist attractions. The first two phases of its construction took it from the newly constructed Whitney Museum on 14th Street north to 33rd Street, to the foot of our south tower. A third phase, opened as we were completing our towers, turned east and passed under the south tower in a covered passage that code required to be at least 60 feet tall.

An unexpected development allowed us to dramatize our response to the High Line. The Coach Company had occupied, since its founding, a building on West 34th Street, the site just blocks away, but the company needed more space. The south tower was offered to Coach but its founder and CEO Lew Frankfurt remarked that he needed a campus, not just floors in a single commercial office building. His comment, and Related's need for its first office anchor, prompted our response. Like the oblique façades, our architectural answer to Coach's needs set a formal precedent that became a basis for further design, an architectural collage of parts and, ultimately, the idea of buildings within buildings.

New York tends to verticalize typologies that elsewhere are horizontal. In our work for Baruch College on the other side of Manhattan, we had verticalized the campus with stairs, elevators, and terraces that served a 13-story atrium. In the south tower, we translated the idea of Baruch's multi-storied campus atrium within a massive building block into a tall volume that we carved into the mass of the tower. Separated from the lower portion of 10 Hudson Yards, and pulled toward the "Shed," the neighboring performance space to the west, the displaced volume—or vertical "campus"—left in its wake a 21-story atrium that gave Coach a void shared by all floors, like an extruded courtyard. From the outside, the atrium, with a façade inset from the surrounding envelope, reads as a gigantic architectural reveal. The reveal outside and void inside consummate an axial view from the High Line.

These are not mute gestures. The displaced volume, reveal, and void engage the surrounding context by reaching out. It was one of the first of our gestures that would turn the buildings into social creatures that talked to others at all heights—in the sky, on the street, and along their shafts.

There are many such gestures in all directions from each of our buildings. Below, the description of these special moments begins at the intersection of 30th Street and Tenth Avenue, and moves clockwise around the perimeter of our structures. I enumerate them individually because the gestures are so specific that, by their nature, they can't be generalized. They are neither duplicative nor normative.

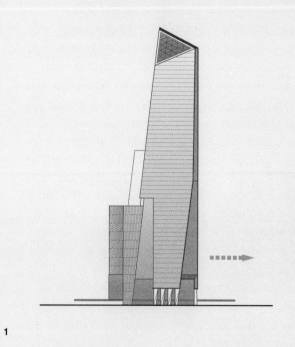

1

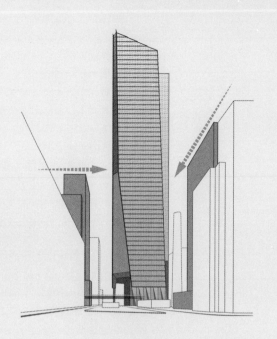

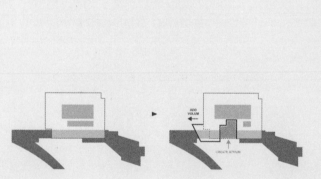

2

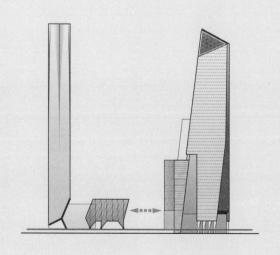

3

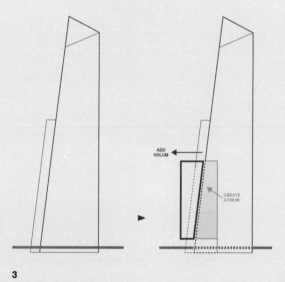

4

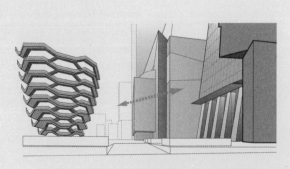

5

1. The southeast corner of our south tower, 10 Hudson Yards, is located at the back of an entry plaza at 30th Street and Tenth Avenue where several urban events occur, demanding architectural acknowledgment. We chamfered the southeast corner at an oblique angle to allow reciprocal views to and from a residential high-rise on 30th St., whose view and light would have been compromised with a right-angled corner that narrowed the street. The diagonal undercutting of the chamfer acknowledges a spur of the High Line passing below, as though making room for its energy. The High Line moves between the building and a colonnade of piers to a terminus that acts as a gathering place that, overlooking the plaza, helps define the plaza below as an outdoor public room.

2. Walking toward the Shed and the Hudson River, we next encounter Coach's tall, trapezoidal atrium, terminating the north axis of the Highline. The 21-story, fully glazed room looks down the entire length of the High Line and further south to the Statue of Liberty. Externally, the soaring space creates an emphatic urban marker that contributes to the legibility of the city.

3. Next comes Coach's 22-story volume, drawn out from the tower's body. The block, its trapezoidal edge complementing the shape of the atrium, anchors the southwest corner of our complex and immediately addresses the Shed to its west by turning toward it. The sharp angle of its north facing side forms a type of sentry for the entrance to Hudson Yards Plaza from the High Line, while marking an individual entry to Coach and to the south tower. The sharpness of its angled external corner reflects the Vessel off in the main courtyard.

4. The Shed leans out as it gestures to our tower. We respond by leaning back. Together the two buildings create a hand-in-glove relationship, one structure inclining as the other reclines. Fully extended, the Shed and our tower compress space framing a view of the Vessel from the High Line and a transitional entry passage into Hudson Yards.

5. On the main plaza, our two towers, 10 and 30 Hudson Yards, bracket the seven-story retail volume. New York architect and glass artist James Carpenter designed its façade to both serve as a backdrop to the Vessel and as a billboard announcing the retail facility. Jamie negotiated, with his monumental west facing sculptured glass surface, (150' high by 300' length), a delicate balance between being discreet and being assertive. Drawing from the horizontal glass shingling of our tower's surfaces, Jamie increased its drama (and dimension) by introducing a concave overlapping scalloped section to each layer of his singles. A tilted plane of glass, which initiates the curving scallop of each layer, angles back to reflect the sky rather than the Vessel, thus avoiding a competitive relationship between the Vessel and its reflection. Images of the sky veil the void of the mall's grand entry atrium while

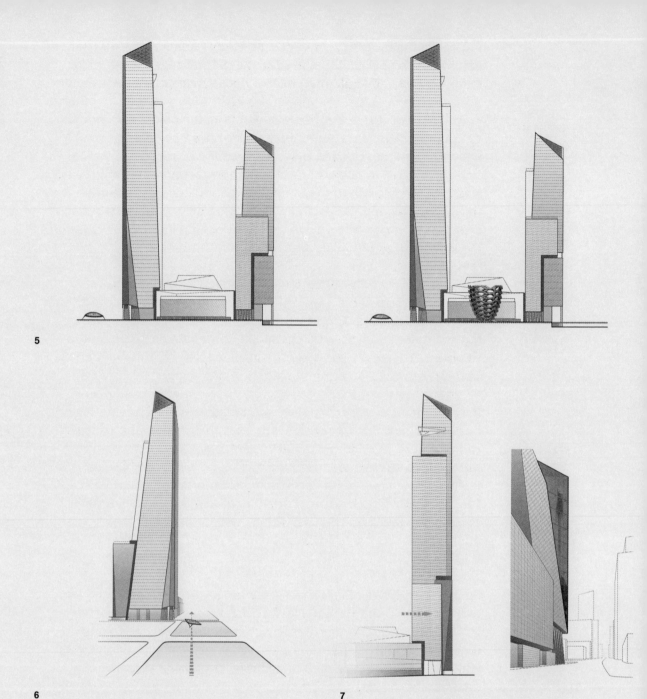

5

6

7

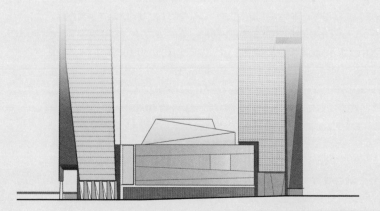

8

still revealing an enticing exposure to the stores inside. At either end of his long, high wall, the glass façade cantilevers past its enclosure revealing the sectional relationship of the glass components.

6. We next encounter the northwest corner, the entry to 30 Hudson Yards, the taller of the two towers. In a gesture of welcome, we positioned the plaza entry on a diagonal to directly face the #7 subway station, undercutting the corner of our tower to create a space of arrival. Two mighty granite-clad columns, tapering as they reach the ground, bracket this monumental porch, and support the chamfered corner of the tower, which soars a full 1,296 feet upward. The corner is an urban marker providing an exclamatory point of reference in the city.

7. The most dramatic corner of our complex, at 33rd Street and Tenth Avenue, doubles as both an entry to the shopping area and the offices. As in other parts of the building, we introduced a mediating volume between the height of the 1,296-foot tower and the street, essentially grafting a smaller building onto the larger, to break down the towering scale. The body of this lower section leans out in *contrapposto* to the tower, which leans back. The two planes of opposing inclination produce the splitting effect of a glacier calving. The drama is accentuated when this corner is seen against the background of the split corners and peeling façades of the south tower. Like the Italians of the Renaissance and baroque periods, I view urbanism as theater. This is the most theatrical event I've directed in a long career.

8. The rotational tour of the complex concludes with the long Tenth Avenue wall of retail, the east-facing counterpart to Carpenter's glass façade facing the inner plaza. This great surface, stretching almost two full city blocks, encloses the east facing, service side, of the retail façade along Tenth Avenue. Here no fenestration is required or desired. Carpenter had scalloped his glass front façade horizontally, and we decided to scallop the back wall vertically, though in a smaller dimension. As a material, we chose perforated stainless steel for its ability to allow the passage of air into the vents behind, and we varied the density of holes punctured through concave scalloping, to texture the wall with variety. A void high on the northern end, intended for a major work of art, interrupts the façade's horizontal scoring, which itself is crossed by diagonal lines that animate the façade and echo all the diagonal lines and oblique planes of the towers. We placed a glass volume at the southern end of the wall where West 31st Street tees off against the building at Tenth Avenue, to announce the wares sold inside like a store window. A blade-like stainless steel canopy, 18 feet above the sidewalk, stretches the entire length of the east facing retail façade. It gives scale to the pedestrian activity along the Avenue and visually binds the separate zones of the volume together. Below the canopy, on its southern end, visual awareness of the retail activity behind is given by an all-glass

10TH AVENUE

33RD STREET

30TH STREET

7

wall modulated by vertical stainless steel projecting mullions. At the northern end the canopy shelters the entrance to the loading facility serving the retail complex.

All the gestures described above were designed to give human scale at street level to otherwise monumental buildings. But we paid as much attention to the upper registers of the building, adding several additional urban gestures along the shafts of the buildings and at the tops, all designed to read from a distance and to conclude the buildings as they meet the sky.

The surface cladding of each of the towers accentuates their stepped massing through textural shifts. Reflective glass surfaces all façades, we combined two types, flat and shingled, smooth and rippled. Their juxtaposition heightens distinctions in the orientation of the towers. The shafts—each with different façade treatments, stepped massing, split corners, the occasional eruptive projection, all set within inclined planes that force perspective—rise to dramatic geometric conclusions: pyramidal volumes sliced on the oblique so that their black voids, like oculi, face toward each other in focused concentration. They would have lost the intensity of eyes locked had they faced away from each other.

One final gesture energizes the urban drama of this dynamic complex. Near the top of 30 Hudson Yards we cantilevered an enormous, glass-sided, glass-floored observation deck 60 feet out into space, gesturing toward the Empire State Building. It was our response to the obvious pairing that occurred when we built a comparably massive super-tall building within blocks of each other: they belonged to one another in the skyline. The architects of the Empire State Building—Shreve, Lamb, and Harmon—introduced the world's first observation deck on a commercial building. Its success inspired hundreds of others. Our gesture pays dramatic homage to that precedent as we reach out into space, somewhat higher, offering the suggestion of conversation, like an architectural annunciation scene.

The construction of this cantilevered deck was unprecedented, a remarkable feat of engineering and construction. The intricate and daring engineering may be hidden from sight, unknown to visitors, but it delivers the thrill of height, and the drama of a breath-taking experience in the thin air of New York's highest altitudes. It is the most theatrical of all our urban gestures. We see it as a gift to the city.

L'ORÉAL

A House on Shelter Island

Shelter Island, New York, U.S. — 2007

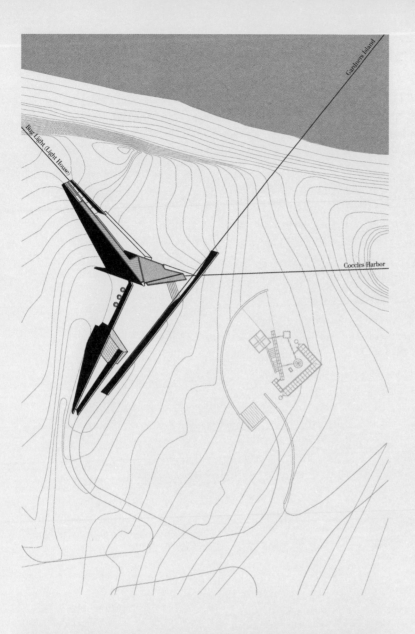

Site and context plan

My wife, Elizabeth, and I purchased a beachfront property on Shelter Island in 1980 with the intention of building a vacation house as soon as possible. We never thought that the design would be my weekend hobby for twenty years. And those twenty years were followed by five more, as I worked with my young associate Andrew Klare in an intensified effort.

Twenty-five years is a long time in an architect's career. Shifts inevitably occur in one's esthetic sensibility. I had taken a bit of a detour during the mid-eighties but once I got back on track, I realized that the house represented an opportunity to bring about a design that came more from my inner core than from external professional influences. Over time the design that emerged was something that could have been sculpted by a receding glacier, or something that emerged out of the sea, like an island. Nature was the inspiration. I was trying to achieve a bond with the land and the land itself inspired an organic answer, through metaphor. I would not be designing an object that sat atop the property but a house that formed a part of it. This felt right to me.

Our property is a three-acre field gently sloping up the side of a bluff that overlooks the ocean. The field is on Little Ram Island, the eastern-most quarter of Shelter Island. To the north, the bluff faces Plum Island and the Orient Point ferry on the North Fork at the end of Long Island. To the northeast, it looks to Gardiners Island, undeveloped but for a single pre-Revolutionary residence. (The island was deeded to the Gardiner family by King of England and still remains in the hands of the family.) To the southeast, we look into the long crescent curve at the near end of Coecles Harbor. Our visual scope is almost 180 degrees. Originally our property was farmed but it has since devolved into a meadow of tall grasses and bayberry bushes that surrounds the house today.

Two neighboring houses adjoin our property (one that I designed twenty-eight years ago). I took care to site our new house so that it would not block our neighbors' views to the same visual landmarks that we valued so much from our property. Only one orientation allowed me to achieve this goal—a diagonal orientation struck along a north-south alignment that embraced the three dominant landmarks—the lighthouse in Gardiners Bay, Gardiners Island, and the entry to Coecles Harbor. The diagonal left the same view shed unobstructed for our neighbors.

The geometry of the bluff, which rises along the water from east to west, initiates the house's form as a spiraling switchback. At the highest point of the bluff, the geometry of the house catches the line of the bluff in the form of a diagonal ramp emerging from the earth, and extends the bluff until it reaches a high point marked by a stone fireplace. There the house pivots again and transforms into a larger volume that extends itself and finally terminates in a cantilever, as though liberated from the earth from which it originated. The switchback gesture links the land and the house in a compositional unity. Natural materials—copper, concrete, stone, wood and glass—make the connection between the natural and built environments, enabling the house to blend with the dominant colors and textures of the site.

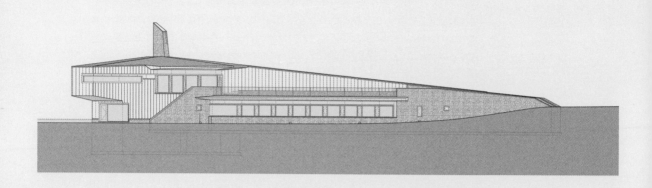

Top: East elevation

Friends who remember my early years as a hockey player sometimes see the geometry of the house as a hockey stick. While it was not my inspiration, the hockey stick is useful as an image that explains the house's composition as a shaft and a blade, the one-story shaft being the wing for sleeping, and the two-story blade, for living.

If the house grew from the land, it takes to the idea of water like a boat. I'm a passionate sailor, and nautical culture influenced its character and the way I think about it. Our classic wooden sailboat, designed by Nathaniel Herreshoff, is moored within sight of our house in Coecles Harbor, and when we approach the house on a driveway that curves back and forth through the waving grass, it seems that we're tacking, as though on a sailboat, through a sea of grass up to another boat, the size of a yacht, itself moored in the grass. The stone fireplace rises like a mast. We let the tall grasses grow, cutting them only in the spring, so from the house, the meadow fuses with the ocean beyond into an undulating surface that moves with the wind. The body of the house narrows and tapers into a prow at the end of the sleeping wing, evoking the idea of a hull cutting through the water. We're on a boat.

The boat imagery continues inside the entry, where high-strength stainless steel cables resembling boat rigging suspend an open-tread, harp-like, split stairway that connects the two main levels in the house's family spaces. Oriented true north to the lighthouse, a large, angular, faceted living/dining room occupies the upper floor, which opens at the far end onto a long tapering deck above the bedroom wing. Below the living/dining area, a combined study/den leads at its far end to a tapering corridor that forms the spine of the bedroom wing. This corridor is a dramatically high, but narrow volume of space that links three bedrooms of diminishing size, each oriented directly toward the sea, the view strafing across the surface of the grasses.

The gesture of the house is dominantly horizontal. Both interior and exterior are woven together by functional elements, such as wood lighting valences inside seven feet off the floor, which have a strong horizontal directionality that ties together all of the interiors from the smallest to the largest spaces. In the upper living area, a forty-foot-long counter joins the kitchen and dining areas with another strong horizontal line. This raised volume is supported by six wood-clad circular columns tensed with stainless rods supporting the main stair.

In the sunken study/den below, a forty-foot horizontal wood built-in acts as a desk on one side and a place for sitting on the other. Within the bedrooms, wood horizontal seating elements directly below the windows link the sleeping areas to the open bathrooms, which focus on free-standing cylindrical glass shower enclosures. Throughout the house, wood-fronted closets provide generous amounts of storage. The interior materials are a carefully chosen blend of fir, stone, and sandblasted concrete combined with plaster ceilings and walls that are left unpainted. Their combination generates a sensuous warmth. The rough sandblasted concrete contrasts with the richness and smoothness of the wood. In the long

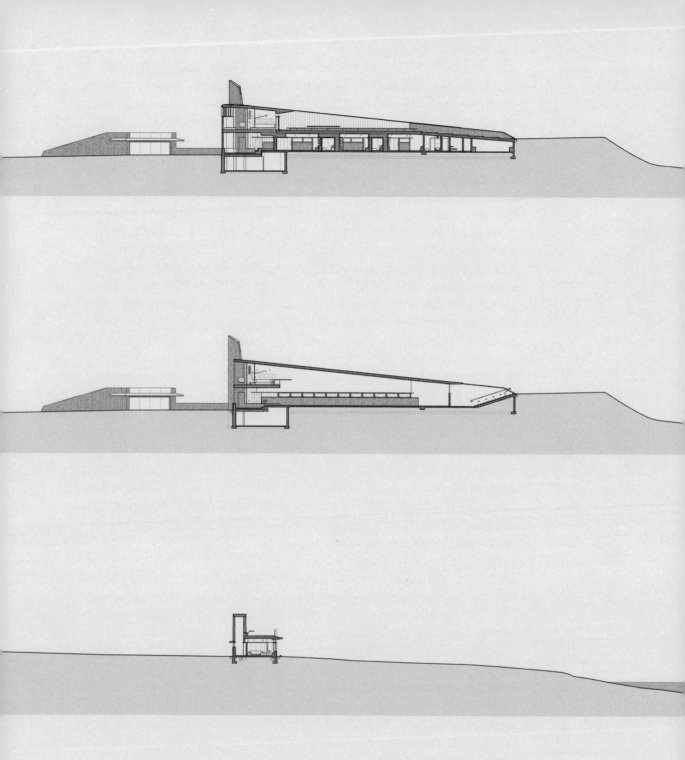

Sections

bedroom corridor, fir runs its entire length of the bedroom walls, and includes two seven-foot sliding panels into each bedroom: when open, the bedrooms connect to the stone-floored corridor and a horizontal run of windows placed at eye height along its entire length. In the summer, the corridor, when opened at either end, circulates breezes through the house that are crossed by air flowing between the corridor and bedroom windows. As a result, the air-conditioning is rarely used.

Outside, extending out onto the deck, a seventy-foot-long stone bench is positioned against a copper wall that encloses the upper volume of the bedroom corridor below. On the opposite side of the long tapering deck, a plane of tempered glass acts as the handrail. Deep horizontal overhangs directly over the glass on the east and west façades shield the house from the sun. On the south façade a series of vertical projecting louvers admit light high into the living room, streaking the main room dramatically in shifting patterns of light and shade.

Designed like a yacht that is yar, where every detail has the utility and esthetic pleasure of brightwork, our house is intended to last. But there is still more to do. After living in it for over ten years it is still not finished. Most of the original furniture is by Hans Wegner and George Cherner, and it has served us well. A dining table and coffee table of my design, and rugs and paintings done by my daughter, Kia Pedersen, specifically for the house, complement the original ensemble. But now that I have become a furniture designer, I intend to furnish the entire house with my designs so that it will truly become a gesamtkunstwerk. You will find the furniture prototypes illustrated at the end of this book.

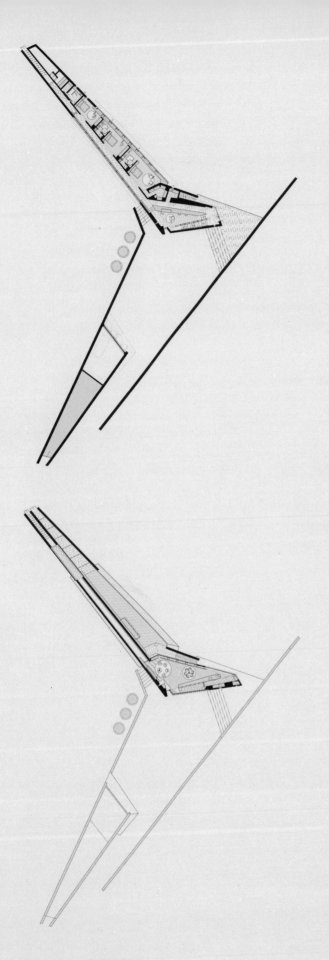

First- and second-floor plan

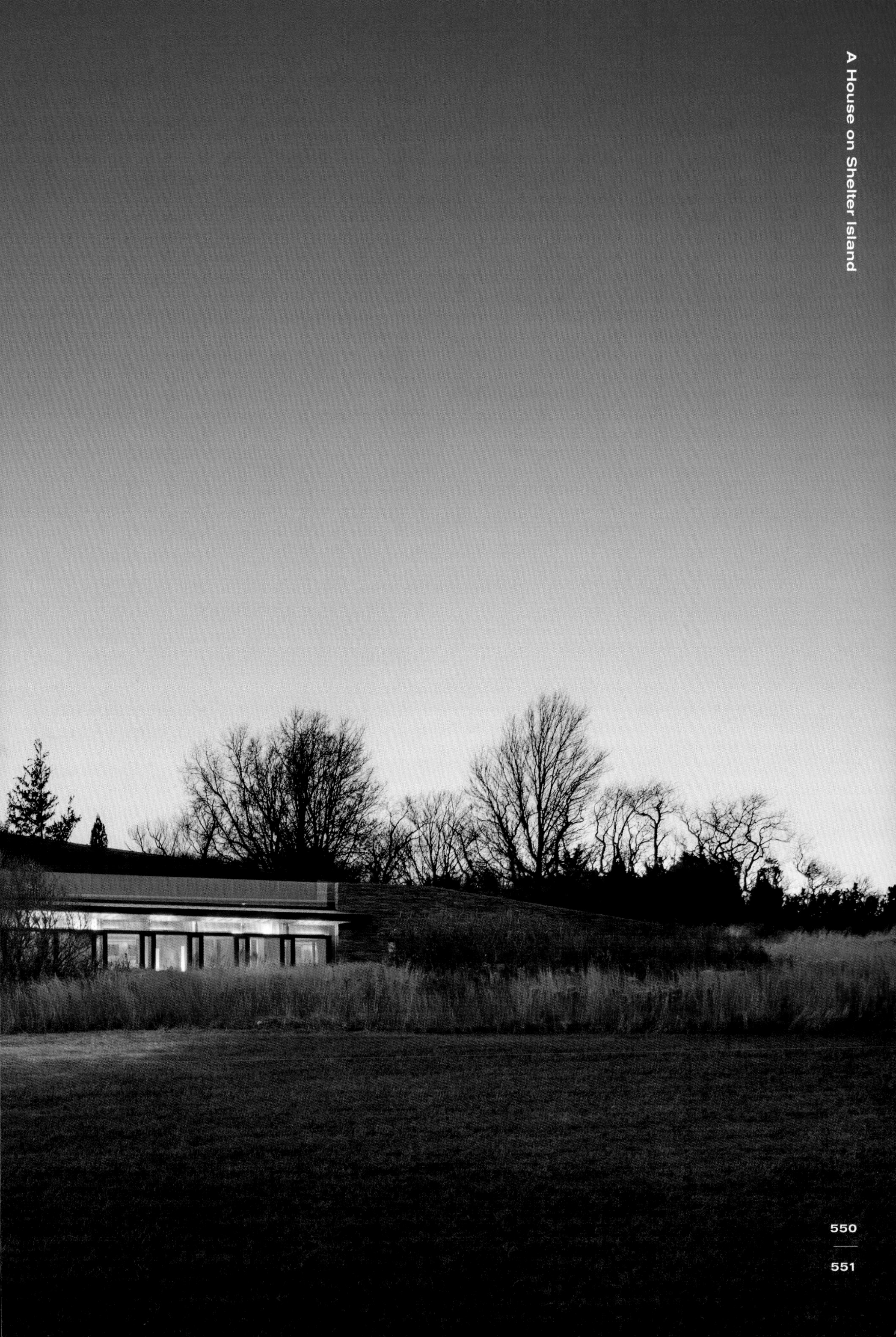

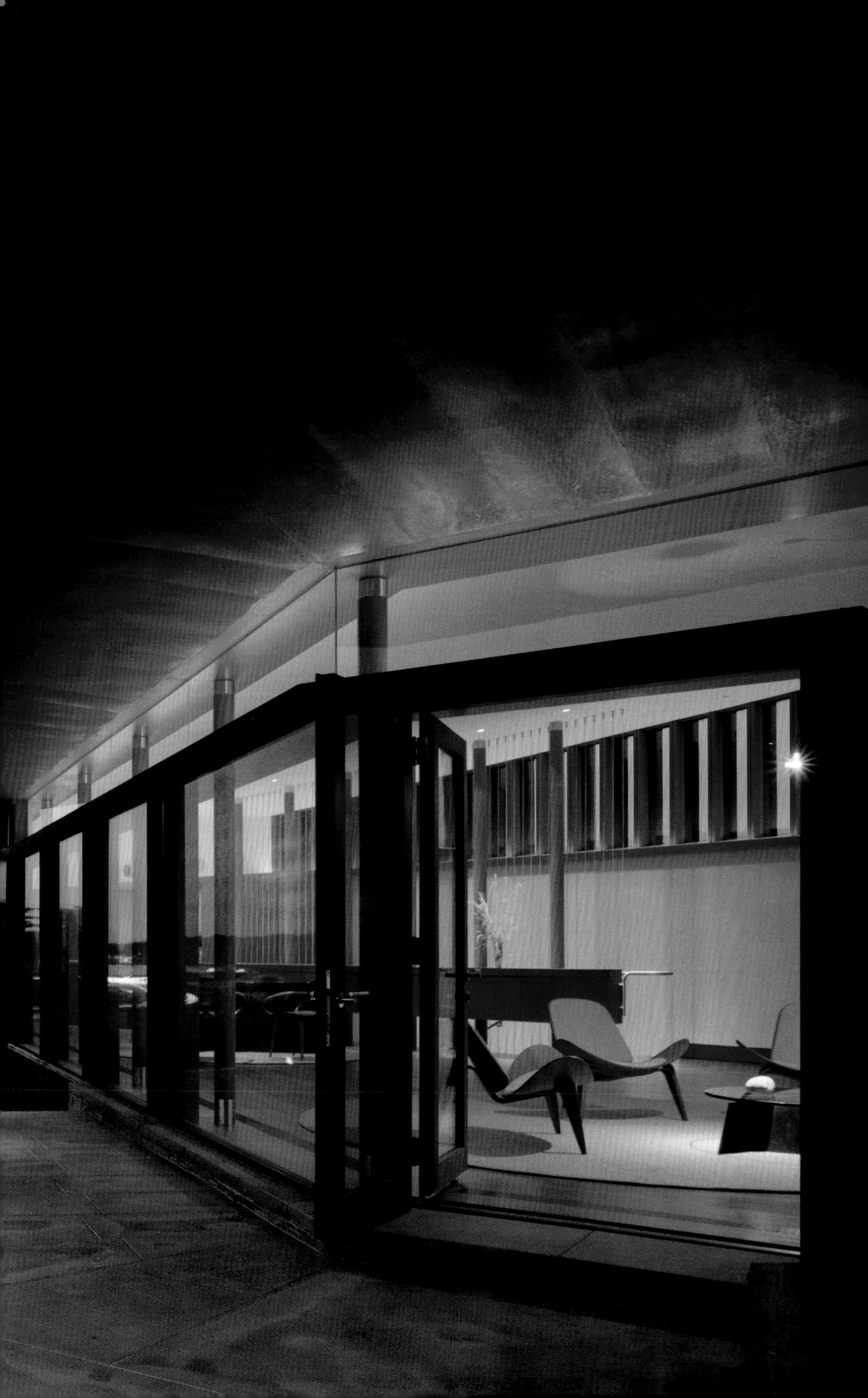

The Chair as Gesture

Despite my belief and emphasis on collaboration throughout my career, I maintain a strong urge to work in relative isolation as an independent artist. After six decades working as an architect, I have turned to the design of furniture as a means of discovering more about myself, focusing on chairs. In an exhibition in Copenhagen I ran across a quotation: "Show me the chairs you design, and I will tell you the type of person you are." In a way, that observation defines my aspiration as a designer: the chair has been the supreme test for many of our greatest architects, the results becoming the baseline against which architects, including myself, measure their ability. Various building types offer different opportunities for architects to reveal their talents, but the design of a chair reduces opportunity to a common denominator and point of comparison.

A chair participates in the architecture of a room. But most often the character of the room in which a chair lands is unknown in advance. The primary factors that influence the design of a chair are not architectural: chairs are seldom site-specific. A chair's dominant role is to interact with the human body. Responding as an architect to the physical forces at work on a design, I find that the chair is an especially rich subject of inquiry. Human comfort is the goal, but so is aesthetic elegance. However, if a chair is not comfortable, a chair is not a chair: it is sculpture. If one wants to do sculpture, why bother with a chair?

Designing a chair solely in response to the architecture of a room makes it a function of architecture, which shortchanges a chair's fuller potential. I know because my earliest attempts fell into that category. They were relatively easy to do. Frank Lloyd Wright did many. The challenge becomes exponentially harder in the design of chairs that both provide physical comfort and embody a personal visual sensibility. The creation of new chair types is extremely rare, but within the evolution of a particular type, the challenge is to invent a stamp of one's own. This is my goal.

My new career, as a furniture designer, was initiated, almost by chance, when I discovered a steel rod lying half buried in a field next to my home on Shelter Island. The design of this home had taken me over twenty years of trial and error. Living in it, I realized that it wouldn't be complete until I designed all the furniture in it as well. Seeing this found steel rod with its beautifully fluid geometry inspired me to try to bend steel into the supporting frame of a chair. I began with material from metal coat hangers, making multiple models of chair types recalling the tubular furniture of the '20s. I discovered, by chance, I could take the type a step further by bending the steel rod into shapes that could, within a single gesture, create all the supporting elements of a chair. I became determined to do the simplest chair possible; one which took the initial tubular steel type developed by Breuer, Stam, and Mies and eliminated all the secondary supporting parts. It became, what I call, my Loop de Loop chair. It is a type of spring, and I consider it an invention of sorts. Joining the frame to a polyester fabric, I created a tension/compression structure of great purity. The evolution and development of it took me six years. Since then, furniture has become a new career. Mies van der Rohe said "a chair takes longer, to design, than a skyscraper."

Which brings me to the point of it all. It's not only the result, but also the process, that now engages me.

Years ago a friend asked Hans Wegner to see what he was working on. He was shown a chair. A year later the friend returned and asked the same question. He was shown the same chair, altered but still in design. Designing a chair is a slow process. At this stage of my career and my life, that is the point. At least in my chair studio, I no longer have externally imposed deadlines. The pace I set is my own. I am assisted in my work by a longtime colleague and friend, Andrew Klare, who works on major KPF projects, and who does the digital translation of my personal exploration into renderings and production code. He brings my two dimensional drawings into three dimensions. He does this while I adjust and modify each step in the process as we work together. While my stated intention was to work as an independent artist, none of this would have been possible without Andrew's great ability.

Now, after seven years, I have developed several chair types. While none has the "invention-like" quality of my Loop de Loop chair, each represents a step in explaining my personal aesthetic sensibility. The surprise is that my second career as a furniture designer explains my first. I discovered that my chairs, done primarily by myself, and my architecture, created in collaboration with many others, have a lot in common.

Uncovering my essential design self within the process of designing buildings and furniture is central to my purpose in undertaking this book, a design autobiography.

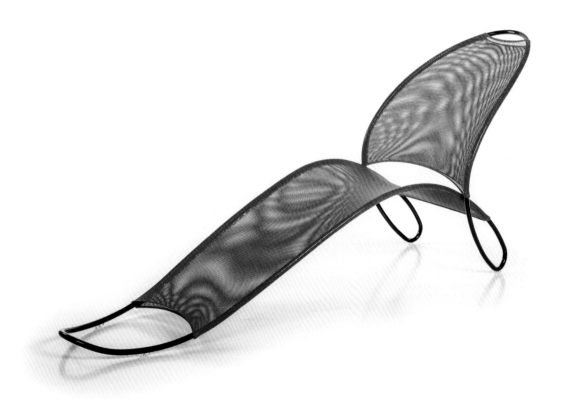

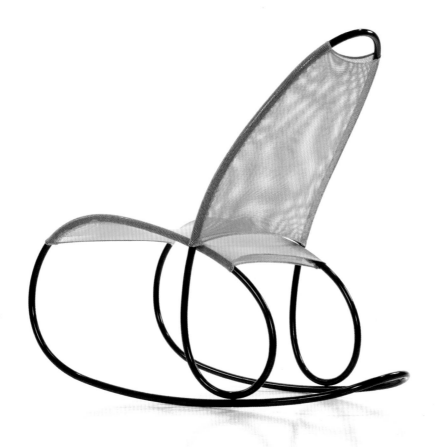

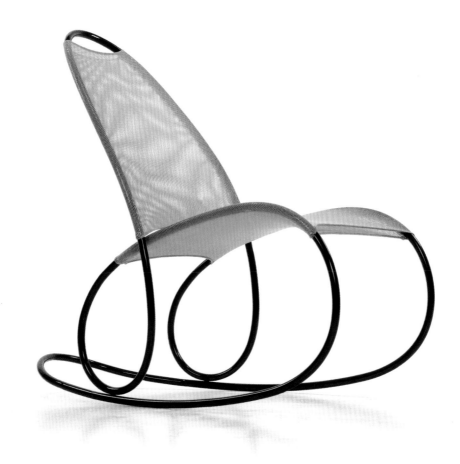

Acknowledgments

Without my partner, Gene Kohn, my career would have taken a very different path. None of the projects documented between the covers of this book would have been possible. Early in my career, I was fortunate to have joined Gene—along with Shelly Fox—in Kohn Pedersen Fox, the partnership we formed at Gene's initiative in 1976. Our close professional relationship continues even after 44 years.

But there have been many other levels of collaboration during those years, for which I am grateful. I am no one-man band. The buildings that follow would have been very different without the talent and dedication of those with whom I worked. My greatest strength may be inspiring and absorbing contributions from others. To a large extent this book pays tribute to the collaborations of KPF's highly professional teams.

In a different way, our clients, too, have been collaborators. They offered not only commissions—some unusual and even inspiring, almost all challenging—but also opportunities for invention. The adage "it takes a good client to make a good building" may be a truism, but the truism, at least in my experience, has proved correct. I am grateful to the many clients for projects that challenged and matured my work and vision. For decades, they have given me the opportunity to think seriously about architecture and to respond responsibly—and I hope creatively—with my pencil.

In the end, it always came down to the hand, yellow trace, and that seminal sketch, but in a context established by Gene, facilitated by my KPF colleagues, and thoughtfully supported by our clients.

Project Credits

333 WACKER DRIVE
Chicago, Illinois
1979–1983
Client   Urban Investment & Development Co.
Architect of Record   Perkins + Will, Chicago, Illinois
Project Principal   A. Eugene Kohn
Design Team Leader   Alexander Ward
Project Manager   Gary Stluka
General Contractor   Inland Construction Company
Structural Engineer   Gillum-Colaco
Mechanical/Electrical Engineer   Environmental System Design

1250 BOULEVARD RENÉ-LÉVESQUE
Montreal, Canada
1988–1992
Clients   Marathon Real Estate, Ltd. and IBM Canada, Ltd.
Architect of Record   LaRose Petrucci & Associés, Montreal
Project Principal   A. Eugene Kohn
Design Team Leaders   Richard Clarke, John Koga
Project Manager   Sudhir Jambhekar
Coordination Leader   Glen DaCosta
General Contractor   Magil Construction
Structural Engineer   Le Messurier Associates/SCI
Mechanical Engineer   St Amant Vezina Vinet Brassard

CARWILL HOUSE
Stratton Mountain, Vermont
1988–1992
Client   William and Carolyn Stutt
Design Team Leader   Josh Chaiken
Project Architects   Alex Bergo, Anthony Mosellie
General Contractor   Peter Laffin

FEDERAL RESERVE BANK OF DALLAS
Dallas, Texas
1989–1992
Client   Federal Reserve Bank of Dallas
Architects of Record   Sikes Jennings Kelly & Brewer, John S. Chase, FAIA
Project Principal   A. Eugene Kohn
Design Team Leader   Richard Clarke
Interior Project Manager   Robert Hartwig
Coordination Leader   Glen DaCosta
General Contractor   Austin Commercial Inc.
Structural Engineers   Charles Gojer & Associates Inc., Datum Engineering Inc.
MEP Engineer   Blum Consulting Engineers Inc.

DZ BANK HEADQUARTERS
Frankfurt, Germany
1986–1993
Client   Agima Aktiengesellschaft für Immobilien-anlage
Architect of Record   Nägele, Hofmann, Tiedemann + Partner
Project Principals   A. Eugene Kohn, Lee Polisano

Design Team Leader   Paul King
Project Manager   Andreas Hausler
General Contractor   Hochtief AG
Structural Engineer   Ingenieursozietät BGS
Electrical Engineer   Reuter & Ruhrgartner
MEP Engineer   Pettersson & Ahrens

FIRST HAWAIIAN BANK HEADQUARTERS
Honolulu, Hawaii
1991–1995
Client   First Hawaiian Bank and The Myers Corporation
Project Principal   Sheldon Fox
Senior Designer   Peter Schubert
Project Manager   Charles Alexander
Interior Project Architect   Barbara Lewandowska
Coordination Leaders   Deborah Booher, Bun-Wah Nip, Kristin Minor
General Contractor   Fletcher Pacific Construction
Structural Engineer   ARUP
Mechanical Engineers   Beall & Associates Inc., Benjamin S. Notkin/Hawaii

THE WORLD BANK HEADQUARTERS
Washington, D.C.
1989–1996
Client   The International Bank for Reconstruction & Development (The World Bank)
Architect of Record   KressCox Associates
Project Principals   A. Eugene Kohn, Sheldon Fox
Design Team Leader   Craig B. Nealy
Project Managers   Thomas Holzmann, William H. Cunningham
Coordination Leader   Joseph P. Ruocco
General Contractor   The George Hyman Construction Company
Structural Engineers   Weidlinger Associates Inc., Weiskopf & Pickworth Consulting Engineers
Service Engineer   Jaros Baum & Bolles Consulting Engineers
Mechanical/Telecommunications Engineer   Flack & Kurtz Consulting Engineers

MARK O. HATFIELD UNITED STATES COURTHOUSE
Portland, Oregon
1992–1997
Client   General Services Administration
Architect of Record   BOORA Architects, Portland, Oregon
Managing Principal   Robert Cioppa
Design Team Leaders   Jerri Smith, Gabrielle Blackman, Douglas Hocking
Project Manager   Sudhir Jambhekar
General Contractor   Hoffman Construction Company
Structural Engineer   KPFF Consulting Engineering
Mechanical/Electrical Engineer   PAE Consulting Engineers Inc.

IBM WORLD HEADQUARTERS
Armonk, New York
1994–1997
Client   IBM
Project Principal   Gregory Clement
Design Team Leaders   Jerri Smith, Douglas Hocking
Project Manager   Christopher Keeny
Coordination Leaders   Gregory Waugh, Simona Budeiri, Charles Ippolito
Construction Manager   Whiting Turner Contracting Company
Structural Engineer   Cantor Seinuk Group PC
MEP Engineer   Jaros Baum & Bolles

GANNETT / USA TODAY HEADQUARTERS
McLean, Virginia
1997–2001
Client   Gannett Company, Inc.
Project Principal   A. Eugene Kohn
Managing Principals   Robert Cioppa, Michael Greene
Planning Principal   Jill Lerner
Design Team Leaders   Jerri Smith, David Lukes
Project Manager/Job Captains   Roger Robison, Takatomo Kashiwabara
General Contractor   The Clark Construction Group
Structural Engineer   CBM Engineers, Inc.
Mechanical Engineer   TOLK, Inc.

THE WILLIAM AND ANITA NEWMAN VERTICAL CAMPUS
Baruch College
New York, New York
1995–2001
Formal name   The William and Anita Newman Vertical Campus
Client   Dormitory Authority of State of New York, City University of New York and Baruch College

Associate Architect   Castro-Blanco Piscioneri
Project Principal   A. Eugene Kohn
Managing Principals   Jill Lerner, Anthony Mosellie
Design Team Leader   Gabrielle Blackman
Interior Project Designer   Mavis Wiggins
Interior Project Manager   Robert Hartwig
Project Manager   Lloyd Sigal
Job Captain   Chris Stoddard
Interiors Coordination Leader   Marta Enebuske
Construction Manager   TDX Construction Corporation
Structural Engineer   Weidlinger Associates Inc.
MEP Engineer   Cosentini Associates

POSTEEL TOWER
Seoul, Korea
1996–2002
Client   POSCO
Associate Architect   Pos-A. C. Co., Ltd.
Design Principal   Peter Schubert
Senior Designer   Kar-Hwa Ho
Project Manager   Chulhong Min
Job Captain   Glen DaCosta
General Contractor   POSEC
Structural & Service Engineer   Arup

SHANGHAI WORLD FINANCIAL CENTER
Shanghai, China
1994–2008
Client   Mori Building Company
Architect of Record   Shanghai Modern Architecture Design Group
Managing Principals   A. Eugene Kohn, Paul Katz
Senior Designers   Josh Chaiken, Ko Makabe, David Malott
Job Captains   Roger Robison, Mabel Tse
General Contractors   China State Construction Engineering Corporation (CSCEC), Shanghai Construction (Group) General Co.
Structural Engineer   Leslie Robertson Associates
Mechanical Engineer   Kenchiku Setsubi Sekkei Kenkyusho

SAMSUNG SEOCHO HEADQUARTERS
Seoul, Korea
2002–2008
Client   Samsung Corporation
Architect of Record   SAMOO
Managing Principals   A. Eugene Kohn, Michael Greene
Design Principal   Peter Schubert
Senior Designers   Thomas Schlesser, Trent Tesch
Project Manager   Lloyd Sigal
Job Captain   Charles Lamy
Construction Manager   Samsung Construction Company
Structural Engineer   Arup
MEP Engineer   Syska & Hennessy Group Inc.

ONE JACKSON SQUARE
New York, New York
2005–2010
Client   Hines
Associate Architect   Schuman Lichtenstein Claman Efron
Managing Principal   Dominic Dunn
Design Principal   Trent Tesch
Project Manager   Lauren Schmidt
General Contractor   Hunter Roberts Construction Group
Structural Engineer   Gilsanz Murray Steficek
MEP Engineer   WSP Flack + Kurtz, Inc.

SCIENCE TEACHING AND STUDENT SERVICES
Minneapolis, Minnesota
2007–2010
Client   University of Minnesota
Executive Architect   Hammel, Green and Abrahamson, Inc.
Managing Principals   Robert Cioppa, Michael Greene
Senior Designers   Jerri Smith, Andrew Klare
Project Manager   Phillip White
Environmental Systems   Tiffany Broyles
Construction Manager   McGough Construction Company, Inc.
Structural & MEP Engineer   Hammel Green and Abrahamson, Inc.

INTERNATIONAL COMMERCE CENTRE
Hong Kong, China
2000–2011

Client   Sun Hung Kai Properties Limited
Architect of Record   Wong & Ouyang
Managing Principal   Paul Katz
Senior Designers   David Malott, Trent Tesch, Eric Howeler
Project Managers   Shawn Duffy, Andreas Hausler
General Contractor   CSCEC + Design
Structural Engineer   Arup
MEP Engineer   J Roger Preston Limited

ROBERT H. JACKSON UNITED STATES COURTHOUSE
Buffalo, New York
2001–2011
Client   General Services Administration-Northeast and Caribbean Region
Managing Principals   Robert Cioppa, Jill Lerner
Senior Designers   Jerri Smith, Trent Tesch
Project Managers   Laurie Butler, Kevin Wegner
Job Captain   Devin Ratliff
Planning   David Ottavio
Construction Contractor   Mascaro Construction Company
Structural Engineer   Weidlinger Associates, Inc.
MEP Engineer   Arthur Metzler Associates

MCCORD HALL
Arizona State University
Tempe, Arizona
2009–2013
Client   Arizona State University
Architect of Record   RSP Architects
Managing Principal   Jill Lerner
Design Director   Jerri Smith
Project Manager   David Ottavio
Design Team   Chad Christie
General Contractor   DPR Construction
Structural Engineer   Meyer Borgman Johnson
MEP Engineer   Energy Systems Design, Inc.

THE OTEMACHI TOWER
Tokyo, Japan
2009–2014
Client   Tokyo Tatemono Co., Ltd.
Architect of Record   Taisei Corporation
Managing Principal   Paul Katz
Design Principal   Josh Chaiken
Senior Designer   Kazuki Katsuno
Project Manager   Shig Ogyu
General Contractor/Structural & Mechanical Engineer   Taisei Corporation

THE ADVANCED SCIENCE RESEARCH CENTER AT THE GRADUATE CENTER AND THE CITY COLLEGE CENTER FOR DISCOVERY AND INNOVATION, CITY UNIVERSITY OF NEW YORK
New York, New York
2003–2015
Client   City University of New York
Managing Principal   Jill Lerner
Senior Designer   Hana Kassem
Project Manager   Phillip White
General Contractor   Skanska
Structural Engineer   LERA
MEP Master Plan Site   AEI Consultants
MEP Buildings   Cosentini Associates

ROSS SCHOOL OF BUSINESS
University of Michigan
Ann Arbor, Michigan
2005–2009 (Phase 1)
2012–2019 (Phase 2)
Client   University of Michigan
Managing Principal   Jill Lerner
Design Director   Jerri Smith
Project Managers   Christopher Keeny, Charles Ippolito, Phillip White, Ted Carpinelli
Technical Coordinator   Phillip White
Design Team   Kenichi Noguchi, Billy Garcia, Lauren Hibner
Interiors Technical Coordinator   David Ottavio
Programming and Planning   Susan Lowance
General Contractor   Gilbane-Clark Joint Venture; Walbridge Construction
Structural Engineer   Thornton Tomasetti
MEP Engineer   Cosentini Associates; AEI Affiliated Engineers

52 LIME STREET
London, United Kingdom
2011–2018
Client   WRBC Development
Architect of Record   Kohn Pedersen Fox
Managing Principals   Dominic Dunn, Charles Ippolito
Managing Director   Paul Simovic
Senior Designer   John McIntyre
Project Manager   Charles Olsen
Senior Architect   Dennis Hill
Technical Coordinators   Luuc Schutte, Maria Banasiak
General Contractor   Skanska
Structural & Mechanical Engineer   Arup

HUDSON YARDS
New York, New York
2008–2019 (Eastern Rail Yards)
Client   The Related Companies
Managing Principals   Paul Katz, Anthony Mosellie
Design Director   Marianne Kwok
Construction Manager   Tishman Construction Company/Tutor Perini
Structural Engineer   Thornton Tomasetti
MEP Engineer   Jaros, Baum & Boles
10 Hudson Yards:
Project Managers   Mark Townsend, Robert Scymanski
Design Team   Robin Fitzgerald-Green, Courtney Higgins, Sameer Kumar, Christina Ladd, Terri Lee, Devon Loweth, Joe Michael, Greg Mell, John Oliver, Heather Ross, Andrew Werner, Justin Whiteford
20 Hudson Yards:
Managing Principal, Retail Interiors   Forth Bagley
Project Manager   Mark Townsend
Design Team   Chad Christie, David Cunningham, Keith Johns, Michael Kirshner, Christina Ladd, Tom McCabe, Anita O'Conner, David Ottavio, Sonal Patel, Chris Popa, Afshin Rafaat, Justin Whiteford, Roy Zhung
30 Hudson Yards:
Managing Directors   Claudia Cusumano, Devin Ratliff
Project Manager   Robert Scymanski
Senior Technical Coordinators   Blanche Nunez, Andrew Werner
Design Team   H Clarke, Hide Furuta, Courtney Higgins, Derek Lange, Ephraim Lasar, Terri Lee, Brendan Lim, Devon Loweth, Joe Michael, Sean Ostro, Mengshi Sun, Josh Triever, Justin Whiteford
Platform/Kiosk:
Managing Directors   Mark Townsend, Robert Scymanski
Design Team   Sujung Choi, Danny Collins, Doreen Danielson, Robin Fitzgerald-Green, John Siderides, Dan Weaver

SHELTER ISLAND HOUSE
Shelter Island, New York
2001–2007
Client   William and Elizabeth Pedersen
Senior Designer   Andrew Klare
General Contractor   Wright and Company Construction
Structural Engineer   Murray Engineering, PC
Mechanical Engineer   Weber and Grahn

THE CHAIR AS GESTURE

Loop de Loop Series:
Design Collaborator   Andrew Klare
Prototype Development   Shea+Latone Inc.
Frame Construction   Fred Sutton of Moiron Inc.
Upholstery   BK Upholstery
Twist Series:
Design Collaborator   Andrew Klare
Prototype Development   Shea+Latone Inc.
Fabrication   Shea+Latone Inc.
Spider Lounge:
Design Collaborator   Andrew Klare
Prototype Development   Shea+Latone Inc.
Fabrication   Shea+Latone Inc.
Upholstery   BK Upholstery
Spider Dining Chair:
Design Collaborator   Andrew Klare
Prototype Development   Henry Elliot
Fabrication   Henry Elliot

Image and Photography Credits

10 Co–founders in New York office circa 1986. Britain Hill for New York Times
16 Courtesy of Kohn Pedersen Fox Associates

333 WACKER DRIVE
25 Barbara Karant
26–29 Hedrich Blessing
30 Greg Murphy
31–32 Hedrich Blessing

DZ BANK HEADQUARTERS
37–40 Dennis Gilbert
41–45 Raimund Koch
46–48 Dennis Gilbert

1250 BOULEVARD RENÉ LÉVESQUE
56 Richard Payne
57 Wayne Nobushi Fuji'i
58 Richard Payne
59 Wayne Nobushi Fuji'i
60–61 Richard Payne
62–68 Wayne Nobushi Fuji'i

CARWILL HOUSE
77–84 Wayne Nobushi Fuji'i

FEDERAL RESERVE BANK OF DALLAS
89–91 Richard Payne
92–93 Vernon Bryant / Dallas Morning News
94–100 Richard Payne

FIRST HAWAIIAN BANK HEADQUARTERS
105–112 Tim Hursley

THE WORLD BANK HEADQUARTERS
121–123 Michael Dersin
124 Tim Hursley
125–128 Michael Dersin
129 Tim Hursley
130–135 Michael Dersin
136 Tim Hursley

U.S. COURTHOUSE PORTLAND
145–156 Tim Hursley

IBM WORLD HEADQUARTERS
161–172 Peter Aaron / ESTO

GANNETT / USA TODAY HEADQUARTERS
181 Michael Dersin
182–196 Tim Hursley

BARUCH COLLEGE VERTICAL CAMPUS
205–212 Michael Moran
213 Jock Pottle
214–220 Michael Moran

POSTEEL TOWER
225–236 H.G. Esch

SHANGHAI WORLD FINANCIAL CENTER
244 Jock Pottle (models)
245–247 H.G. Esch
248–249 Mori Building Co.
250 Shinkenchiku
251 H.G. Esch
252 Shinkenchiku
253 Jimmy Lin
254–255 Shinkenchiku
256–259 Tim Griffith
260 Mori Building Co.

SAMSUNG SEOCHO HEADQUARTERS
269 Jae Seong Lee
270–271 H.G. Esch
272 Jae Seong Lee
273–288 H.G. Esch

ONE JACKSON SQUARE
293–297 Raimund Koch
298–299 Michael Moran
300 Raimund Koch
301–305 Michael Moran
306 Raimund Koch
307-308 Michael Moran

SCIENCE TEACHING AND STUDENT SERVICES
317–321 Tim Griffith
322–325 Peter Sieger
326–332 Tim Griffith

INTERNATIONAL COMMERCE CENTRE
340 Jock Pottle (models)
341 Tim Griffith
342–343 Coloursinmylife / Shutterstock
344–345 Nacasa & Partners
346–347 Tim Griffith
348 Grischa Rueschendorf
349 Tim Griffith
350 Grischa Rueschendorf
351–353 Tim Griffith
354–355 Sean Pavone / Shutterstock
356-359 Tim Griffith

U.S. COURTHOUSE BUFFALO
369 David Seide
370–371 Biff Hennrich
372–373 David Seide
374 Biff Hennrich
375–380 David Seide

MCCORD HALL
389–401 Tim Griffith
402 Douglas Salin
403–404 Tim Griffith

THE OTEMACHI TOWER
412 Jock Pottle (models)
413–428 Nacasa & Partners

ADVANCED SCIENCE RESEARCH CENTER
430 Tim Griffith
437 Tim Griffith
438–439 Jeremy Bittermann
440–441 H.G. Esch
442–444 Jeremy Bittermann
445 H.G. Esch
446–447 Jeremy Bittermann
448–449 Tim Griffith
450–451 Jeremy Bittermann
452 Tim Griffith
453 H.G. Esch
454 Steve Hall / Hedrich Blessing
455 H.G. Esch
456 Tim Griffith

ROSS SCHOOL OF BUSINESS
458 Aerial Associates
462 Axons by KPF
465 Tim Griffith
466–467 Barbara Karant
468–475 Tim Griffith
476–477 Raimund Koch
478–480 Tim Griffith

52 LIME STREET
489 Guy Archard
490–491 John Bushell / KPF
492 Antoine Buchet
493 Morley von Sternberg
494 Hufton + Crow
495 Alex Upton
496 Hufton + Crow
497 Morley von Sternberg
498–499 Tim Soar
500-501 Hufton + Crow
502 Tim Soar
503 Hufton + Crow
504 Tim Soar

HUDSON YARDS
506–512 Illustrations by Kohn Pedersen Fox Associates
514 Axon illustration by Martin Tang / KPF
517–518 Michael Moran
519–525 Connie Zhou
526–529 Michael Moran
530–538 Connie Zhou

A HOUSE ON SHELTER ISLAND
542 William Pedersen
547 William Pedersen
548–562 Michael Moran

CHAIRS
565–574 Hub Wilson
575 Kristine Larsen

ACKNOWLEDGMENT
576 John Chu / KPF